DATE DUE			
10/26/98			
12/13/99			
3/27/02			
11/15/02			
MAR 30 2015			

Colonial American Craftspeople

Colonial American

CRAFTSPEOPLE

by Bernardine S. Stevens

680

COLONIAL AMERICA

FRANKLIN WATTS

NEW YORK / CHICAGO / LONDON / TORONTO / SYDNEY

Frontispiece: A colonial weaver

Photographs copyright ©: Historical Pictures/Stock Montage: pp.
2, 18, 51, 96; The Bettmann Archive: pp. 14, 16, 22, 28, 38, 41, 43, 47,
49, 53, 59, 62, 68, 71, 75, 76, 80, 86, 100, 104, 107, 108; Henry Francis
du Pont Winterthur Museum: p. 25; New York Public Library,
Picture Collection: pp. 30, 33, 65, 90, 93; North Wind picture
Archives, Alfred, ME: pp. 34, 91.

Library of Congress Cataloging-in-Publication Data

Stevens, Bernardine S.
Colonial American craftspeople/by Bernardine S. Stevens.
p.   cm.—(Colonial America)
Includes bibliographical references (p.   ) and index.
Summary: Describes the training and work of such craftspeople
as carpenters, masons, silversmiths, wigmakers and
leatherworkers living in the American colonies.
ISBN 0-531-12536-X
1.Handicraft—United States—History—Juvenile literature.
2. Artisans—United States—History—Juvenile literature.
3. United States—Social life and customs—to 1775—Juvenile
literature. [1. Handicraft—History. 2. Artisans—History.
3. Occupations—History. 4. United States—Social life and
customs—to 1775.] I. Title. II. Series.
TT23.S75 1993
680'.0974'09032—dc20   93-19323 CIP AC

Contents

AUTHOR'S NOTE   9

ONE   11
    **APPRENTICES: CRAFTSPEOPLE
IN TRAINING**

TWO   20
    THE WOODWORKERS

THREE   31
    THE BUILDERS

FOUR   45
    **PAPERMAKERS, PRINTERS,
AND BOOKBINDERS**

FIVE   57
    THE METALWORKERS

SIX   88
              **FASHION COMES TO
                THE COLONIES**

SEVEN   103
              THE LEATHERWORKERS

SOURCE NOTES   110
GLOSSARY   111
BIBLIOGRAPHY   116
FOR FURTHER READING   121
INDEX   123

This book is dedicated to teachers everywhere

AUTHOR'S NOTE

The most difficult part of writing this book was limiting its length. It was hard to write an overview of colonial craftspeople when there were so many different occupations. I've chosen to present woodworkers; builders; papermakers, printers and bookbinders; metalworkers; fashion workers; and leatherworkers. Colonial gunsmiths, shipbuilders, tailors, weavers, millers, glaziers, shoemakers, and saddlemakers—to name a few—were active craftsworkers, too. But often these trades were offshoots of the ones described here. For example, a blacksmith might have adapted his knowledge and skills to gunmaking, or a goldsmith might have become a locksmith. Shipbuilders had to know carpentry and joinery before they could repair or build ships. I believe the crafts I've selected had the greatest impact on the development of colonial life.

The chapter on fashion is included for a different reason. It is important for students to know that colonial women sometimes did work outside the home. Girls could become involved in a family business when there was a shortage of workers. And women were known to take over businesses upon the death of their husbands, as several women printers in Maryland and Virginia did. But apprenticeships for girls seem to have been limited to the fields of millinery, dressmaking, or related domestic trades.

One more thing. Although this book is written in the past tense, master craftspeople today still use the techniques, tools, and materials of the American colonial craftspeople. That's why they are called masters.

Bernardine S. Stevens

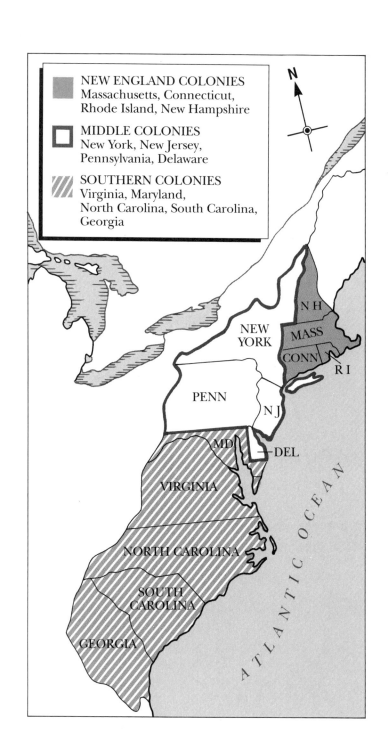

NEW ENGLAND COLONIES
Massachusetts, Connecticut,
Rhode Island, New Hampshire

MIDDLE COLONIES
New York, New Jersey,
Pennsylvania, Delaware

SOUTHERN COLONIES
Virginia, Maryland,
North Carolina, South Carolina,
Georgia

N

N H

NEW
YORK

MASS

CONN

R I

PENN

N J

MD

DEL

VIRGINIA

NORTH CAROLINA

SOUTH
CAROLINA

GEORGIA

ATLANTIC OCEAN

CHAPTER ONE

Apprentices: Craftspeople in Training

Starting a new life in early seventeenth century America was not easy. Lack of proper food, poor medical care, and severe weather are a few of the things that killed many settlers. Despite these brutal conditions, people wanted to move to the young colonies. Not all of them were humble people who desired religious freedom. Many new arrivals dreamed of owning businesses, land, and homes. Those who didn't have the money for their passage to the colonies often signed contracts called indentures. As indentured servants, which included children, they agreed to work for the individuals who paid their passage. Children indentured to artisans were called apprentices.

As the colonies became more established, the courts or the parents of the children apprenticed the youngsters to craftspeople to learn a trade. They continued to sign a type of indenture that stated what was expected from both the master and the apprentice during the bondage period.

An apprentice vowed to keep any trade or other secrets his master showed him. He promised to be loyal to his master. He said he wouldn't lie about his master or allow others to speak badly about him. He swore he would not leave his master's service without permission, even for one day. He promised he wouldn't buy or sell anything that belonged to him or his master without permission. He pledged he wouldn't gamble or go to taverns, alehouses, or playhouses (theaters). Finally, the apprentice swore he wouldn't get married or be guilty of any immoral behavior for as long as he served his master.

The master promised to teach his apprentice the art and mystery of his craft. He was to ensure that the youth learned to write and do arithmetic, if capable. At the end of the servitude, the master usually gave the apprentice a set of tools and any other freedom dues, or terminal gifts, that had been set forth in the indenture. As long as the young person stayed in his service, the master was to provide him with food, clothing, and a place to sleep.

Until the American Revolution, there was little difference between colonial and English indentures. However, in the colonies, the number of years an apprentice had to serve did vary.

Original colonial indentures were based on English municipal laws and laws adhered to by English guilds. Guilds were organizations similar to modern trade unions. They ensured their members had completed extensive training and *earned* the right to be called master craftspeople. Two specific English laws, the

Statute of Artificers of 1563 and the Poor Law of 1601, set the standards and practices accepted and enforced by guilds and local authorities.

The Statute of Artificers was written to provide inexpensive, semiskilled labor for craftspeople. The Poor Law of 1601 dealt with the guardianship and support of orphans and poor children. Although this second law did not state that a craftsperson had to train his "pauper apprentice," the majority of artisans did provide this education for their wards.

These laws had several things in common. Both stated that an apprentice was bound to a master by a recorded indenture. The servitude period was to be a minimum of seven years. However, girls could be released from their indenture by marriage. These laws established that a master was to treat his apprentice like his own child.

Similar laws were enforced in the colonies. For example, in Virginia, the Poor Law of 1672 authorized the county court to apprentice poor and illegitimate children whose parents could not afford to raise them. Officials believed they were preventing these children from becoming vagabonds, ruffians, or drunkards. In 1619 this same procedure had been used by the Virginia Company to bring one hundred orphans from the streets of London to the colonies, where their indentures were quickly purchased. The venture was so successful it was often repeated, and not only by the Virginia Company.

By 1621 it was difficult for craftspeople in the sparsely populated colonies to find apprentices. The great demand for help during the seventeenth century led to children being trepanned, or kidnapped, in English seacoast towns. In time, corrupt authorities made a lot of money by participating in the growing practice of kidnapping of children and adults. Some kidnapped children transported to the colonies never saw

One of the most famous colonial apprentices
is Benjamin Franklin, who was apprenticed
to his brother, James, a printer.

their families again. Trepanning and the speedy purchase of indentures show how desperate colonial craftspeople and others were to get apprentices and servants.

There were no child labor laws in the seventeenth and eighteenth centuries. Children worked as soon as they were physically able. If authorities felt that a child knew what he was doing and could sign or mark an indenture, the contract was legal, regardless of the child's age. Generally, a child was apprenticed at fourteen. One unusual case is that of Gabriel Muray of Yorktown, Virginia. His mother bound him at the age of one to John Richardson, a carpenter and joiner. The boy's indenture read that he was to serve until "the full age of twenty-one."

In an ideal situation, when a colonial boy turned fourteen, his parents found a kind master craftsperson to teach the youth the trade he wanted to learn. For the next four to seven years, the apprentice worked diligently. He learned all he could, and he helped his adopted family around the house. After his servitude, he received his freedom dues of land, an ax and a hoe, some Indian corn or tobacco, and perhaps some money. He then stayed on with his master as a paid journeyman. When he earned enough money, he opened his own business as a master craftsperson. Maybe he even married his ex-master's daughter and taught his craft to apprentices of his own.

Things didn't usually happen this way, however. The child's feelings were seldom considered when his parents chose a trade for him. If he were the oldest son of a craftsperson, he generally learned and then inherited his father's business. Younger sons were apprenticed to any craftsperson who needed or wanted them.

The master filled an apprentice's days with work from sunrise until sunset. The youngster rose early in the morning and completed household chores before

While the master tailor measures his customers,
the apprentices cut and sew in the workroom.

leaving for his master's shop. When it was dark, he
returned to his master's home, did his evening chores,
ate, and worked on his reading or arithmetic before
going to bed. On Sundays, if the master was pious, the

lucky apprentice got to spend all day in church. Apprentices who worked outdoors often got a reprieve if the weather turned bad.

Girls who were apprenticed worked as hard as boys. It would be more accurate to refer to these young women as indentured servants. They were seldom taught a trade unless it had to do with some type of domestic work. They learned to sew, cook, and run a home—skills that prepared them for marriage, not careers. Girls who didn't act like "ladies" were sent to the fields to work. They were fortunate if their masters taught them to write or do math. Since the lives of most settlers revolved around religion, girls were taught to read and study the Bible. Yet even those girls not apprenticed rarely attended school. When a young lady's term of service was over, she received freedom dues, which usually consisted of Indian corn or tobacco, perhaps a new set of clothes, and some money. Quite often, girls would marry before the official end of their bondage.

The lives of apprentices could be very difficult. Long hours filled with hard work, beatings, and poor food and shelter sometimes led to death. Few people thought a master was wrong to beat an apprentice, and if the apprentice ran away, he could be severely punished.

Perhaps a runaway would be forced to wear a "pot hook" when he was captured. Today someone wearing this iron collar might be considered a radical dude. To a colonist, it was a sign of shame. An apprentice who "absented himself from his master without permission," could receive other punishments. In some colonies a captured runaway might have been whipped. Or he might have had to work additional time to repay his master for money spent in trying to recover him. This might have included money for advertising, paying a

Many crafts were performed at home,
such as spinning yarn and making candles.
These products were also offered for sale
by professional craftspeople.

reward, the expenses of the people returning the runaway apprentice, and anything that he might have stolen when he ran away.

To keep runaways to a minimum, colonial legislators created laws to protect apprentices and allow them to voice grievances against their masters.

Just as an apprentice was required to stay with his master, a master was obligated to remain in one place and teach his ward. If he failed to do this, he was penalized. Unusually cruel masters could be, and were, punished. One documented case involved a boy who was brought to the colonies from England. He became very ill with scurvy and was in poor health because, "His master used him with continual rigor and unmerciful correction."[1] When the boy died as a result of this treatment, his master was hung. Another incident in New England involved Judith Weekes. She admitted to causing the death of her husband's apprentice by cutting off his toes. Not all cases were this severe. A female servant in Virginia was dunked for disrespect. Her master was also dunked because he failed to maintain proper authority over her.

If an apprentice's complaints were found to be true, he could be removed from one master and placed with another. The laws written in the colonies protected both the apprentice and the master from violations of indenture obligations. The courts were generally fair to both parties.

Thousands of people came to the colonies as indentured servants. Many took advantage of their freedom dues and went on to become prosperous citizens. Their children and grandchildren fought for freedom and helped to create the United States. Americans should feel great pride as they talk about these industrious people, for many of them are descendants of indentured servants.

CHAPTER TWO

The Woodworkers

The first woodworkers to arrive in the colonies were undoubtedly overwhelmed by the acres of forests they saw. Coopers couldn't count the number of barrels they'd make. Joiners envisioned miles of paneled walls and wooden floors. Carpenters' hearts pounded as they thought of the many houses they would build and how quickly they would return to England as rich men. None of these people was realistic. No one prepared them for the harsh winters or the challenges of daily existence in the new land. They found their talents often had to be used in different ways. Coopers and joiners were asked by fellow settlers to make simple, utilitarian furniture. Carpenters frequently discovered coffin making was their chief source of income.

Woodworkers used a variety of hand tools—axes, saws, hammers, mallets, chisels, gouges, files, clamps, and braces. The same equipment is still used by modern woodworkers. Today's tools, however, often are made completely of metal. Those of the colonists were made of wood, except for metal cutting edges. An example would be the plane.

The plane is a tool used to smooth and shape boards and other wooden surfaces. The size and type varies according to its use. Basically, the colonial plane was a block of wood with a metal cutting edge and a wooden handle. The floor models used by the colonists were just larger pieces of wood with bigger cutting edges. A modern floor plane hums as electricity moves its multiple blades. Colonial woodworkers would be shocked to see how fast today's electrical tools do the work it took them hours or days to complete.

COOPERS

All woodworkers were important to the colonists. But it was most likely the cooper, or barrel maker, who first established his trade in the new world. By law, every ship going on a long voyage had to employ at least one master cooper. His job was to care for the ship's casks, which held its drinking water and provisions. This meant the first ships to land in America had coopers on board. Since much of what the colonists used, shipped, or traded was stored in barrels, the paramount need for coopers cannot be overlooked.

The colonial cooper worked with several woods. White oak and hickory were chosen for barrels that held liquids. These woods are strong, heavy, and non-porous. Cedar and pine were used for household items like buckets, tubs, and churns. They are soft woods and easy to shape. Ash, another popular choice, is light and flexible, yet tough. Coopers could work quickly with it to produce many items.

A cooper, or barrel maker, forces a trussing ring
over his barrel. Staves, trussing rings, and bands
clutter the floor of the workshop. Huge calipers
used to draw barrel heads hang ready for use.

In teaching an apprentice, a cooper might have
first shown him how to split timbers from the center of
straight trees. Using a broadax, a short-handled ax
with a wide edge, he shaped timbers into rough staves.
The center part of the stave was wider than its two
ends. The cooper finished tapering and shaping the
staves on his jointer. The jointer, a large plane, was
often secured to the floor of the cooper's shop. Its
razor-sharp cutting edge was exposed, which allowed
the cooper to draw staves across it.

Turning from his jointer, the cooper laid the staves in a circle. If he used newly made staves, they were still "green." This meant they bent easily. To make them more flexible, the cooper heated or steamed them. He forced one end of each stave into a gathering ring. He then placed hickory trussing rings over the staves, pushing them together into a tight circle. The trussing rings were replaced by iron bands made by a blacksmith or tin bands made by a whitesmith. The very first coopers sometimes relied on permanent bands made of strong leather.

JOINERS AND CABINETMAKERS

Although coopers could make basic furniture, it was more important for them to produce as many barrels as possible. For this reason, it was usually joiners who made furniture in the colonies. Joinery is the craft of fitting pieces of wood together to make floors, paneled walls, window frames, doors, and furniture. However, the first people to arrive in the colonies had no need for paneled walls and intricate floors. They were concerned with simply staying alive, not building fancy houses.

By the late seventeenth century, English joiners had learned to make lighter, more decorative furniture of European design. Some of them formed a guild and began to call themselves cabinetmakers. Others continued to call themselves joiners even if furniture making was a major part of their business. Another group of these craftspeople chose to concentrate only on joinery. Many English cabinetmakers brought their new designs to America.

With the arrival of additional craftspeople to the colonies, life became less of a struggle. People had more time to make money and to participate in leisure and social activities. As colonists developed more of a social life, they wanted to live in more pleasant surroundings. Practical, sturdy furniture had served its purpose. People now wanted attractive, more decorative furniture. Men and women both enjoyed having comfortable chairs and sofas. Women liked to have tea tables for serving their guests. People were reading and writing more, so they wanted bookcases and desks. Even their freestanding closets, called armoires, were built by cabinetmakers. Paneling around doors, windows, and fireplaces became more ornamental. The joiners' and cabinetmakers' bank accounts grew with the demand for beautiful flooring, paneling, and furniture.

By 1730, major furniture manufacturing centers began to appear in the colonies. Philadelphia, Pennsylvania, was the largest, followed by Newport, Rhode Island, and Charleston, South Carolina. English kings, queens, and their cabinetmakers influenced colonial designs. Thomas Chippendale's book, *The Gentleman and Cabinet-maker's Director*, became an important guide for colonial furniture makers. The colonial cabinetmaker would add his own touches to Chippendale's designs to make his piece truly one of a kind. By the mid-eighteenth century, British cabinetmakers felt the competition from the colonies. British exports to the colonies declined as people showed a preference for American-made products.

An American cabinetmaker could personalize his product by simply choosing to use his favorite wood. One artisan might prefer mahogany. Another would choose walnut, cherry, or maple for the same design. All cabinetmakers developed a knowledge of every wood. Each knew how to capture the beauty of the wood's grain in the final product.

An apprentice cabinetmaker who appreciated the beauty of wood had the enthusiasm it took to become a master. By learning geometry and mathematics, he de-

A display of colonial furniture at the Henry
Francis du Pont Winterthur Museum shows
a variety of woodworking techniques. Solid,
utilitarian furniture was replaced by lighter,
more decorative furniture toward the end
of the seventeenth century. The ceiling
design of joists and summer beams
is discussed in chapter three.

veloped a sense of proportion and form. He studied
different styles of design and ornamentation, from an-
cient Greek to Chippendale, so he could design his own
furniture. When an apprentice applied the engineer-
ing principles he studied, the furniture he built as a
master was perfectly balanced and stayed strong.

Apprentices also learned a lot about lathes. These machines rotate a furniture maker's work horizontally. As a lathe turns, a fixed cutting tool presses against the work to shape it. The master's hands are then free to guide the cutting tool along his piece rotating on the lathe.

If the master used a treadle lathe, he provided the power. He tied one end of a heavy cord on the foot treadle, or lever, of the lathe. The other end was tied to a spring pole attached near the ceiling. His work was supported on tapered rods called centers. Pressing down on the treadle with his foot caused the work to spin against the cutting tool and bend the pole downward. When he released pressure on the lever at the bottom of his stroke, the pole was pulled back up. The work paused until the treadle went back into place. A master cabinetmaker developed a steady rhythm as he worked on his treadle lathe, hardly noticing the pauses.

The great wheel lathe was used to make crown moldings, millwork, and turnings. It had a wooden wheel about six feet around with a crank on its axle. A belt running from the rim of the wheel drove a small pulley on the lathe. This delivered a steady high-speed spin to the work. The master guided his work, providing the downward stroke. He made repeated passes with the cutting tool. When the piece was completed, it had a wavy finish. Power for this lathe was usually provided by an apprentice. Donkeys or oxen were also used to run these lathes. A few cabinetmakers may have found them easier to train than apprentices!

After deciding what to make, the cabinetmaker chose the primary wood for the outside of the piece. He selected the best finish for that wood. Then he picked a cheaper secondary wood to build the inside parts. The most important decision was how to best show the beauty of the wood's natural grain.

After the woods were chosen, each part of the design was separately cut and shaped. These pieces were joined together to make the final product. The apprentice who heard his master refer to "joints" knew the cabinetmaker wasn't talking about the local tavern or body parts. In furniture making, joints are the points at which the pieces of wood are fitted together. They are the foundation of sturdy furniture. No one would buy a wobbly dining-room table. A chest with imperfect joints could completely fall apart. And so might the reputation of the cabinetmaker who made it.

Many joints used by colonial cabinetmakers were used by carpenters and other woodworkers, too. In fact, modern woodworkers still use them, and many more. They included mortise and tenon, dovetail, lap, and butt. Mortise and tenon joints were made by cutting a tenon, or peg, at the end of one piece. The second piece had a matching slot or groove, called a mortise, cut into it. The tenon was slipped into the mortise to make the joint. This joint was very useful for fitting secondary woods at right angles.

The dovetail joint was a different type of mortise and tenon joint. Its tenon was shaped like a dove's spread tail. The mortise was cut out of the part to be attached. Cabinetmakers used dovetail joints when making drawers.

Lap joints were made by cutting the ends of two pieces of wood to one-half their thickness. Then they were laid over one another. Butt joints were squared ends of timbers fitted together.

A cabinetmaker took pride in the perfection of his joints. He *may* have strengthened them with warm glue made from boiled animal bones and skin. Occasionally, he might have driven a wooden peg into a joint to make it stronger. The true craftsperson used metal nails or screws only when attaching hardware, like hinges, to

In a cluttered workshop, a cabinetmaker applies glue to slats for a chairback. Other chairbacks hang on the wall, while samples of his cabinet work, possibly patterned after Chippendale, surround him.

his furniture. He always used caution when making a joint. A poorly made joint could ruin the primary wood's pattern, or worse, cause a piece of furniture to be unstable.

The finish used on the furniture often depended on the cabinetmaker's personal taste. He could either stain the wood or buff it to a high gloss.

Stain contained a dye that deepened the wood's natural color. This brought out the pattern of the wood's grain. Powdered chalk could be added to the stain to fill any pinholes in the wood.

Before a finish was applied, the wood was sanded. Next it was stained, then sanded again. Finally, a coat of varnish or shellac was brushed onto the wood. Varnish was made by dissolving copal resin from tropical trees in turpentine. Shellac was made by dissolving in alcohol a secretion from an insect called a lac. When the furniture was dry, it was sanded again. This process was repeated until the piece had a high glossy surface.

The craftsperson then had the option of waxing the stained furniture which would seal the finish. The cabinetmaker mixed melted beeswax with turpentine. He brushed the hot mixture onto the furniture. The craftsperson completed the procedure by polishing the waxed wood.

A blend of linseed oil and turpentine could also be used to finish the wood. This mixture was poured onto the surface of the piece, wiped off, and then allowed to dry. The cabinetmaker then buffed or sanded the piece. A patient cabinetmaker repeated this technique for hours until his hard work and the image of his face were reflected by the finish.

To complete the piece, the cabinetmaker added iron, brass, or wooden knobs, and other hardware, as needed.

Early woodworkers were versatile. A cooper could serve as a carpenter or sawyer. A coachmaker might

Shipbuilding required the skills of many craftsworkers: hewers, sawyers, caulkers, coopers, carpenters, joiners, and others. Shipsmiths made the ironwork. Sailmakers and ropemakers used their skills, while tinsmiths made the lanterns. In all, it could take twenty to thirty craftspeople a full year to build one ship.

also be a chaisemaker or carver. A cabinetmaker or carpenter could do upholstery work and serve as the town undertaker.

Regardless of their specialty, woodworkers have always had one thing in common: the desire to turn wood into a masterpiece that could last a lifetime or longer.

CHAPTER THREE

The Builders

Construction apprentices did a lot of work out-doors. They heard the chirping of birds mingle with the pounding of hammers and the scraping of the bricklayers' trowels. They enjoyed the smell of freshly cut wood in the crisp morning air. If the weather turned bad, most of them had work they could do indoors. They had the best of both worlds. These young craftspeople knew it took hard work and dedication to become master builders.

It took time for construction craftspeople to develop their trades in the colonies. Their talents weren't required to construct the temporary shelters of the first colonists. The homes of these settlers were not made of brick or stone. They had no glass windows. Architects did not design them. Some of the first colonists lived in holes in the ground covered with brush. A number of them quickly erected replicas of the lodges Native Americans used for their homes. Others built simple houses of wattle and daub without professional assistance.

Wattle and daub had been used in England since the Middle Ages. A house made this way consisted of an uncomplicated wooden frame that could be built by people without carpentry skills. The wattle roof was formed by weaving twigs together. The house and roof then were covered with daub, a mixture of mud, straw, and clay.

Eventually, other colonial immigrants constructed buildings similar to those in their home countries. The Dutch built narrow brick houses with stepped roofs. They imported most of the brick from Holland. The log cabin was introduced by the Swedes. It could be built by one man who had nothing more than an ax and trees. This house required no hardware. Its popularity was spread by the Germans who showed the Scotch-Irish how to build them. Log cabins could be seen in the colonies long after wattle and daub dwellings had disappeared.

ARCHITECTS

As the seventeenth century drew to a close, the new colonial middle class wanted homes that reflected their good fortune. At the same time a great interest in architecture had developed in England. This resulted in the publication of many books on the subject. When men with some training in architecture started coming to the colonies, they brought books with them that covered every subject from structural designs, plans, and styles, to the building trades.

Soon every proper gentleman was expected to have some knowledge of architecture. And many American aristocrats designed their own houses. It was important that they understood the information in the architectural books. If they didn't, and if they hired poorly trained craftspeople, the results could be disastrous.

Early settlers cooperated in home building.
Nails were usually not available, so wooden
pegs called trunnels were used instead.

However, teams of novice American architects and
master craftspeople did create elegant buildings that
continue to impress students of architecture.

Professional craftspeople were rare in the South, so
in the southern colonies, plantation owners often hired
master builders from England to construct their
homes. These men had served long apprenticeships.
They took pride in their workmanship and were quali-
fied to supervise other craftspeople.

Owning a piece of land was only one factor to be

Trained surveyors measured land
holdings, prepared maps, and marked
boundaries. The colonial surveyor in this
old illustration is George Washington.

considered when deciding to build a house. The land-
owner, who often served as the architect, and the
builder had to decide what type of structure could be
erected on a particular site. Then they designed it.
Next they determined what materials would be used in
its construction. Wood, clay, and stone were the ones
most commonly used during the colonial period. Once

the materials were chosen, actual construction started by digging a hole for the foundation. This was called excavation.

MASONS

After the land was excavated, perhaps a mason arrived to lay the foundation. Masonry is work performed using stone, rock, brick, and marble. Colonial brick masons or bricklayers made and worked with brick. Stonemasons worked with stone and brick. Marble masons worked with all types of masonry materials but displayed their greatest dexterity working with marble.

Stone and marble masons knew that one incorrect strike with the chisel could shatter a valuable piece of stone. To avoid this, they taught their apprentices to work with the grain of the stone, rock, or marble.

The master also taught his apprentice when to use different masonry materials. An apprentice who went on to specialize in stone carving—the craft to which many of the intricately carved colonial archways, statues, and columns can be attributed—usually worked with limestone. This stone is formed underwater from the shells and skeletons of marine organisms. It is easily carved.

A master mason could transform any rock or stone into a useful building material. Rock is harder and stronger than limestone and was used to build foundations, walls, and fireplaces in colonial structures. There was plenty of rock just lying around. But it was also cut from the face of a rock quarry by masons. The quarried rock usually required only minor "dressing," also known as "facing," on the construction site.

A mason dressed a stone depending on his employer's wishes. Stone and marble can be rough- or smooth-faced. Rough facing entails trimming away only enough projections from the stone to allow it to be properly laid in a straight line.

When a stone was to be rough dressed, the first tool the mason used was his mashing hammer. One end of this tool resembles a mallet. The other end is an extremely sharp and tempered blade. The hammer weighed about three pounds. In using a mashing hammer, the mason relied on his swing and rhythm, not his muscular strength. When he hit the targeted projection with the cutting edge, chunks of stone would fall to the ground.

Next the mason would place a "square" over the stone. This L-shaped measuring tool is used by many craftspeople. Colonial stone and marble masons used it for marking straight lines on materials they were dressing. After scratching the line on the stone, the mason used either a coping tool or a pitching tool. Both resembled chisels. The coping tool was used mainly by marble masons to achieve perfectly squared edges. The pitching tool was used more by stonemasons when they were rough dressing a stone.

The mason held his pitching tool on the line and swung his mallet. When the mallet struck the pitching tool, pieces of stone flew through the air. He continued removing unwanted bulges of stone using the pitching tool and mallets of different weights.

Smooth facing was done using mallets and a "point." The point resembled an ice pick and enabled the mason to remove very tiny projections. It was possible for him to end up with a perfectly flat, rectangular stone.

After the mason dressed his stones, he would "pull a line." This was a string tightly tied to two stakes. One stake was placed at each end of the proposed wall. The craftsperson relied on the line to determine the length and height of the wall. He also used it to keep the top of his wall straight. As he went along, the mason used true artistry to develop his wall. To do this, he followed several rules. He never laid in a row more than four or five stones that were the same size, shape, or thickness. He concentrated on one small section of the wall at a time. He laid the back stone first, then the front. He filled spaces with small stones. His greatest accomplishment was dressing rocks to fit together so perfectly they required no cementing material. This was called a dry wall. When needed, he added mortar to hold the rocks in place.

The slang term for mortar is mud. In colonial times it was a dry mixture of lime and sand reinforced with animal hairs. The mason added just enough water to form a ball. Then he molded the mortar around the rocks and allowed it to dry. He completed laying the foundation a foot or two above ground. Now the home owner had the colonial version of a frost-free refrigerator. The cellar stayed cool year-round.

BRICKLAYERS

Foundations, walls, and chimneys were some items made from brick as well as stone or rock. Bricks were easier to work with than stone or rock because they were one size and shape. They didn't have to be dressed. They were small and easy to handle. By combining bricks and stones, colonists could build structures such as arches and vaults.

Colonists made all bricks from clay. Clay is a common mineral substance made up of very small rock particles. It is frequently mixed with other substances such as sand and silt. Clay was readily available throughout the colonies, especially in lake and riverbeds. When it's wet, clay is easily shaped. When it's dry, it's hard and stonelike. At temperatures of about 850°F,

While the master bricklayer works
from a scaffold, his apprentice has
the task of preparing mortar.

it changes chemically and no longer turns to mud when wet.

Colonial bricklayers sometimes mixed animal hair or straw with clay to hold it together and strengthen it. Water was added to the clay, and it was blended until it had an elastic texture. This mixture was put into wooden molds and air dried for several days. The dried "green" bricks were removed from the molds and baked in ovens called kilns. At 1,000°F, the clay turned a different color.

The color of brick could range from nearly white to red or reddish-brown to dark purple or blue. The color depended on the amount of iron and other impurities in the clay as well as the method of baking the brick. The color darkened as the temperature rose.

Like other masons, the bricklayer first pulled a line. He then laid his bricks in a horizontal layer called a course. His mortar was mushier than a stonemason's and was applied with a trowel. This is a flat-bladed tool with a wooden handle. The thin horizontal and vertical layers of mortar between bricks are called joints. Stronger walls are built by having the vertical joints of one course stand in the centers of the bricks below. The bricklayer used a light pressure to set his course. He tapped bricks into alignment with the handle of his trowel.

Since it was important that a wall or chimney be straight, the mason placed a spirit level on top of each course to ensure that the bricks were properly laid. The level had a clear tube that held alcohol or some other liquid. The liquid contained an air bubble. If the course was even, the air bubble stayed in the center of the tube. If the bubble was not centered, the mason knew he had to make adjustments to the wall.

Additional bricks and mortar were carried to the bricklayer in a hod. This resembled a small trough with one open end and was mounted on a long pole. It was usually carried over the shoulders of the bricklayer's apprentice.

HEWERS AND SAWYERS

Before sawmills were built in America, a carpenter often relied on a hewer to provide his timbers.

The hewer did his job standing on a log that was laid and secured over two smaller logs. Although a few saws were available in the early settlements of some colonies, the hewers relied on their broadaxes to shape timbers.

First, the hewer cut and chipped pieces of wood from one side of the log. The last series of chips were hewn away from the timber with an adz. This was a very sharp ax shaped like a hoe. It left the surface of the timber very smooth. After the hewer repeated this process on four sides of the log, he had a squared timber.

When saws were introduced to the colonies, the hewer developed into a sawyer and teamed up with a pitman. They squared logs and cut timbers over a pit. Each one held one end of a long pit or sash saw. The sawyer stayed on the topside of the log. He enjoyed the sun and fresh air as he guided the saw along a chalk line he had marked on the log. Meanwhile, his partner worked in the pit providing the downward stroke of the saw. He got covered with sawdust. Certainly more than one pitman's wife fussed at him for getting so dirty.

When the sawyer and the pitman had enough timbers prepared, they contacted the carpenters.

CARPENTERS

The carpenters whirled into action when constructing a building. First one group placed a heavy wooden sill

Hewers, in the foreground, work on
squaring summer beams, while the master
builder directs carpenters and other workers.

on top of the foundation wall. Another crew was kept
busy shaping posts.

They shaped a tenon at the bottom of each post,
and a mortise was cut into the top. The post was tempo-
rarily placed into one of the mortises that had been cut
into the sill. A hole was bored into the post's tenon and
the sill. Then it was laid aside while another post was

shaped. Tenons were also carved into each end of beams called girts. All of the mortises and tenons were marked with corresponding numbers. The carpenters would match these numbers to ensure the proper fit of the joints.

After all the posts and girts were prepared, two walls called broadsides were constructed. Broadsides were assembled by fitting a girt over posts. They were raised into place using poles called pikes. When the front and back broadsides were in place, carpenters secured the end girts to them. The tenons of the posts were secured in the sill with wooden nails.

Next, a gigantic beam called a summer was put into place. It ran the length of the building. Its tenons were placed into mortises that had been cut into the end girts. The summer supported horizontal timbers called joists. The joists served two purposes. A floor could be nailed to them, and they could be left exposed to provide a ceiling for the room below. While joists were being installed, another crew of carpenters could be placing studs. Studs are vertical timbers used to fill out the wall frame. Nogging was stuck between the studs to provide insulation. Early nogging was rolls of straw held together with clay. In the later colonial period, stone and clay or brick and mortar were used. As the nogging was being placed, the master was supervising the building of the roof.

The roof's frame was provided by timbers called roof rafters. They were connected by several long timbers known as purlins. In the early colonies, light poles were fastened across the rafters. Bundles of straw were lashed to them in overlapping rows. These thatched roofs could last thirty years—if they didn't catch fire.

By the mid-seventeenth century, roofs began to be covered with boards ranging in length from one and a half to three feet. Originally the boards were overlapped. Eventually, carpenters discovered it was better

A carpenter in his shop prepares a wooden
board by planing it. Saws and gouges
hang within reach above the workbench.

if the boards were shaved flat and tapered with a draw-knife. People who specialized in this type of work were called shingle-makers.

As a house neared completion, finishing touches like fancy flooring, paneling, door and window frames, molding, doors, windows, and hardware were desired. And when people wanted them, even more craftspeople were called upon to provide them. Sawyers, pitmen, joiners, cabinetmakers, glaziers, carpenters, and different smiths could all make money. There's no doubt, it took many craftspeople to make a house a home.

CHAPTER FOUR

Papermakers, Printers, and Bookbinders

Thomas Carlyle, a Scottish historian and essayist, wrote, "May blessings be upon the head of Cadmus, the Phoenicians, or whoever it was that invented books." Writers, publishers, and teachers nod in agreement. They cheer his words. Students groan, wince, and mutter different opinions. Yet they are the lucky ones. They can read and study an abundance of printed material. Very few books were available to early colonial children.

Initially, most colonial books came from England. As Americans began to have more free time, they wanted newspapers and books for education and entertainment. They needed paper to conduct business. But the British government controlled what was printed in the colonies by limiting printing supplies and paper exported to America. By the early 1700s, several colonial papermills were trying to fill the demand for paper.

PAPERMAKERS

One major problem early papermakers had was collecting rags to make their product. Colonists usually put their rags to other uses.

Apprentices, called ragpickers, started the papermaking process by separating cotton or linen rags into piles. The rags were soaked in water and allowed to rot. The rotten rags were then beaten by the huge wooden hammers of a stamping mill. The rotting and the pulverizing caused the fibers of the cloth to break apart. The loose fibers, called stock, were washed and stored in chests.

Each morning the ragpickers filled a large vat with stock and water. When this tub was full, the vatman lowered a mold into the solution. The mold was a screen with a removable wooden edge called a deckle. After filling the mold, it was shaken. The liquid was sifted through the screen. The shaking caused the fibers to cross over one another. As they settled on the screen, they formed a sheet of paper.

The vatman then removed the deckle and passed the screen containing the sheet to a coucher. After draining more water from the sheet, the coucher flipped it onto a woolen or felt cloth and returned the screen to the vatman.

The coucher and the vatman worked together until they had a post. This was a pile of one hundred and forty-four sheets of paper individually separated by cloths. Excess water was squeezed from the post by a

A woman delivers rags to the papermill,
while the craftsman displays the final product.

hand-screw press that was powered by every worker in the shop. If too much water remained in the paper, it would be of poor quality.

After the post was removed from the press, a layboy or layman separated each piece of paper from its cloth. The paper was lightly pressed several more times and hung to dry.

The surface of the dried paper was porous and had to be "glazed." This prevented ink from being absorbed into the paper's surface. The papermaker could glaze the paper by burnishing it.

Burnishing was done by rubbing the paper's surface with a fine-grained stone. If done improperly, burnishing ruined the paper's appearance by streaking it. An alternate method of finishing the paper was called sizing.

In sizing, the paper was dipped into a warm gelatin made by boiling animal hides, hooves, and bones. The gelatin filled the paper's pores. After the paper dried, it was pressed with great force under a plating hammer. Because the hammer's surface covered an entire sheet, the pressing resulted in an even finish. At last the paper was ready to be used by the printer.

PRINTERS

Early colonial printers didn't enjoy freedom of the press. A printer's license could be revoked for criticizing the government. The church, often a printer's biggest customer, would stop sending him work if he printed something that it considered to be offensive. He could be at risk if he dared to print opinions that differed from those of the general public.

Adding to this craftsperson's headaches were the limited supplies of available type and paper. A large book could take years to publish if the printer had to

The techniques and tools used for papermaking
were the same in the American colonies as
those shown in this etching of a papermill
from a French encyclopedia of 1764.

A. The vatman dips his mold into the stock vat.
G. The coucher removes the paper from the
screen as he prepares a post for the large
hand-screw press.
H. The press used for squeezing excess water
from the post
I. A layboy arranges a stack of paper for
further pressings.
L. The planishing hammer

wait for paper from England. The printer would produce what he could and store it until more paper arrived. Authors who lived far from printers were unable to proofread the rough printed drafts of their work known as galley proofs.

There are many errors in early American books. If mistakes were made, they usually remained. It was too expensive and time-consuming to do reprints. Master colonial printers did the best with what they had; but if a printing job had no time limit, London printing houses were used.

Adequate help was another area of concern for the printer. Apprentices, called devils, ran away, and journeymen printers traveled to find work. Sometimes a printer used unskilled labor at the press. If the shop offered bookbinding services, they were usually done by the master's wife. Customarily, women were assigned to this craft. Some colonial wives followed the European custom of taking over the management of printing shops when their husbands died.

Few early printers specialized in one trade. They were often writers, editors, publishers, postmasters, compositors, and pressmen. People could also purchase stationery supplies, small groceries, medicine, and even fiddle strings from these craftspeople. Their political influence was evident when they refused to print articles or pamphlets contrary to what they believed.

To do his job, a printer would use pieces of type. Type was a single letter of the alphabet, a number, or a symbol made from metal. No one made type in the early colonies, it had to be imported. Eventually type foundries were established in America, but the demand for type was always greater than the supply.

The compositor was the man who set the type. He would read a handwritten copy of what was to be printed as he pulled the appropriate pieces of type

Letterpress printing was a slow process. The form had to be re-inked frequently to ensure quality print. The compositor's case for holding the type pieces can be seen in the background.

from his "case." The case was a shallow tray divided into two main sections, upper and lower. It was subdivided into smaller sections containing the individual type characters. The letters were not arranged alphabetically. The ones used most often were closest to the compositor.

Type was set into a hand-held frame called a composing stick. It held one line of type. Blank pieces of brass were placed between letters and words to space the line to its desired length. These composite lines were then transferred to a flat tray called a galley. A galley contained one page of print. It was inked, and a galley proof was printed.

After corrections were made from the galley proof, the composite lines were moved to a flatbed of stone or wood. The type was locked into a metal frame called a chase. The set pages locked in the chase were called the form. The printer tapped the type with a piece of wood to make sure it was level. After this was done, the form was ready for the press.

The colonial method of printing, called letterpress, was done on a sheet-fed press. These presses were made up of different-size frames and rails. The form was secured in a frame called a coffin and inked with two leather balls stuffed with wool. The coffin was pressed by a platen against one sheet of paper at a time. Letterpress printing was slow. It is easy to understand why books were such treasured possessions to the colonists. Often, however, readers cared as much or more about a book's binding as they did about its content. It wasn't long before craftspeople specializing in bookbinding opened shops.

BOOKBINDERS

The materials used by colonial bookbinders were the same as those used since the earliest days of printing: wooden boards or stiff pasteboard, coverings, glue, thread, and simple tools for decorating leather.

The bookbinder started by folding the printed pages into sections. Each section was sewn through the fold and attached to the one above it by a chainstitch. When the sections were all connected, the bookbinder decided what type of cover to put on it.

Flexible vellum was a favorite covering for record books. A bookbinder would use blue or marbled paper

THE

HISTORY

OF THE

First DISCOVERY

AND

SETTLEMENT

OF

VIRGINIA:

BEING

An ESSAY towards a General
History of this COLONY.

By WILLIAM STITH. *A. M.*
Rector of *Henrico* Parish, and one of the Governors of
William and *Mary* COLLEGE.

Tantæ molis erat *** condere gentem. Virg.

WILLIAMSBURG:
Printed by WILLIAM PARKS, M,DCC,XLVII.

A sample of colonial printing from 1747

for unimportant books and pamphlets. Schoolbooks were covered with thin boards of oak or birch called scabord, or scaleboard.

Very special books were bound in wooden boards covered with leather. The bookbinder would place a wooden board on the front and the back of the book. Then he pulled the ends of the sewing cord through holes in the boards. He molded a dampened leather cover over the boards and secured it to the wood with glue. This step also hid the stitched spine of the book.

The final step in bookbinding was the decorating of the leather cover. A true craftsperson didn't rely on fancy tools or supplies to produce superior work. Heated irons pressed into the dampened leather produced beautiful designs. Sometimes a fillet was used to decorate the cover. This was a small hand-held tool that had a wheel with an edge engraved with a repeating design. The bookbinder rolled it over the cover of the book to produce the desired effect. Sometimes one or two of the book's edges were coated with gold or silver. Or the edges of a book's pages could be dyed to match the color of its binding. Even precious jewels and metals were used to decorate particularly important volumes.

Reading material varied according to the location of the colony. In New England, people were likely to learn to read for the purpose of studying the Bible. This gave them an advantage in gaining a formal education. Most of them felt learning was both a duty and a privilege.

In the middle and southern colonies, the higher economic class automatically received an education. Their libraries were more political and literary than religious. They regarded reading as a source of pleasure with a useful purpose. It enabled them to exchange ideas and philosophies.

In 1699, Cotton Mather wrote a book called, *A Family Well-Ordered*. It had a subtitle two paragraphs

A colonial-style bookbindery

long! In it, he advised parents, "the Children of Death, and the Children of Hell, and the Children of Wrath, by Nature, need much parental guidance to overcome these handicaps." In the second half of the book, directed toward children, Mather warned in bold black print, that children who "made light of their parents" would "suffer the wrath of God." It's no wonder that colonial children were afraid to express their true feelings.

Entire books glorifying the deaths of "godly" children were thrust into the hands of healthy, normal ones. A book published in 1717 was called, "A Legacy for Children, being Some of the Last Expressions and Dying Sayings of Hannah Hill, Junr. Of the City of Philadelphia, in the Province of Pennsylvania, in America, Aged Eleven Years and near Three Months." This book is a morbid account of Hannah's death. She became terminally ill and spent the last days before her death in bed. She passed the time preaching and giving moral advice to her family and friends. Her words were recorded and published as the "Ardent Desire of the Deceased."

America has achieved greatness through the printed word. Men and women struggled, fought, and died to defend the First Amendment. And although students may groan, wince, and mutter opinions different than writers, teachers, and publishers, in their hearts they are cheering Thomas Carlyle.

CHAPTER FIVE

The Metalworkers

Smith is a common last name. It is also a person who works with metal. All colonial smiths worked with some kind of refined metal. Their tools and techniques were often identical, although they may have used different names for them. A forge or hearth was standard equipment in their shops. Apprentices got plenty of exercise pumping bellows to keep fires burning hot. Colonial smiths pounded and shaped metals with the same expertise they used to help mold America's future.

Metals used by the colonists had common characteristics. They were opaque and capable of being shined to a luster. They conducted heat well. They could be fused. They were malleable, meaning they could be rolled or hammered without breaking. They were also ductile, because they could be drawn out, bent, or hammered into thin sheets.

Colonial smiths knew some metals were more limited in their uses than others. These metals were alloyed to make them more useful. An alloy is a mixture of two or more metals. Alloys can also be a metal and a nonmetal substance blended together.

Colonists found some metals in a pure state. Others had to be extracted from their ore. This was done using a fusing process called smelting. The metals were then refined before being used. The settlers removed impurities from metals by heating them to a molten state. Sometimes a fluxing, or cleansing agent, like borax, was used in the refining process. Other times, fluxing was not necessary. After the colonial smith refined his metal, he usually shaped it into bars for storage.

Before they could be shaped into a product, most metals had to be softened. This was done by heating them in a forge. A colonial smith's forge was square or rectangular in shape. It was made of stone or brick. The fire bed was hooded to carry smoke and fumes to the chimney. A set of bellows was used to direct blasts of air onto the hot coals to intensify the heat. The smith added fuel to the fire as it was needed. To do this, he used a long-handled, lightweight shovel called a slice. Hot coals were packed around the outside of the fire to prevent heat from escaping. A type of rake called a fire hook was used for removing burnt fuel from the forge and adjusting the burning coals. To decrease the heat, the smith would shake water onto the fire using a bunch of twigs called a washer.

Regulating the fire was essential. It had to be large enough to accommodate the work being done. Yet a fire that was too large wasted fuel. The hot spot of the fire had to be close to the draft of the bellows. But if it were too close, it could be scattered by a powerful blast.

It was also important for the smith to know when his metal was ready to be worked. Smiths didn't have thermometers on their forges. They judged how hot their metal was by its color. A blood-red heat was used when only the surface of the metal had to be worked.

An old drawing of a blacksmith's shop
in colonial Vermont shows a full
array of the craftsman's tools.

White heat was used if the metal was to be formed, shaped, or drawn out. A "sparkling or welding" heat was used when pieces were to be joined together. If the metal got too hot, the smith would dip it into water or an acid until it reached the right color. Then he swiftly and accurately hammered the metal before it lost its heat.

As the smith forged his metal, occasionally the constant heating, rapid cooling, and reheating caused it to become brittle and crack. The smith would then anneal it. To do this, he would heat the metal and allow it to cool slowly and naturally. Through this process, the smith tempered, or hardened and strengthened, his metal. Sometimes tempering was intentionally done, such as when a smith was forging various tools or cutting blades.

Most preliminary forging was done on an anvil of some type. In colonial America, anvils could be large blocks of metal, with or without "horns" and "heels." Or they could be small accessory ones called stakes. These were oddly shaped and used in a variety of hammering processes. Each one had a spike on its bottom that allowed it to be fitted into a large anvil or a workbench.

Metalworkers used two types of hammers: hand and sledge. Hand hammers were held in one hand; the work was held in the other. The hammers ranged from tiny ones used in clock making to forge hammers weighing two to four pounds.

Sledges were large hammers that had to be swung with both hands. Smiths used up-hand sledges to draw out or batter metal. They were rarely lifted above the head. "About" sledges were the biggest hammers used on the largest work. They were lifted above the head in a full swing.

Of course, not every metalworker used every hammer. For example, an ironworker would have little use for a tack hammer. And it is doubtful that a gold-smith pounded his delicate metal with a twenty-pound sledge.

Tongs were another tool commonly used by colonial smiths. Tongs had different-shaped mouths, which enabled them to hold different-shaped pieces of hot metal. Straight-nosed tongs were used when working with small flat pieces of metal or metal plates. Crooked-nosed tongs held bars and thick objects. Pick-up tongs were for general use.

Shears were used for cutting metal. They ranged in size from the small, hand-held type to ones so large they were secured in a workbench or on the floor. These huge shears could be closed only when the full weight of the craftsperson was exerted on them. Flasks were frames used for holding sand molds. Punches, blunt metal rods, were used for repoussé and hole punching. Gravers, tools with stubby handles that held V-shaped blades, were used for engraving. Saws, chisels, files, swages, vises, calipers, and sometimes even lathes, could round out a smith's tool set. Each set was as individual as the smith who used it.

A colonial smith usually started work by heating a bar of metal and pounding it with a hammer into flat sheets or plates. This initial process was referred to as battery. Smiths used other hammering processes such as raising, hollowing, planishing, and drawing out. The angle at which the hammer hit the metal determined if the metal's thickness remained the same, increased, or decreased.

Raising stretched the metal in an upward direction. It was used in the making of tankards, mugs, and a multitude of similar products. Hollowing was often used together with raising. It was accomplished using hammers and anvils. This term also referred to the process of hammering out sheet metal, cutting it ac-

A Native American blacksmith's
shop of the colonial period

cording to a pattern, and soldering the pieces together
to make things like cups.

Planishing was a finishing process. The smith used
a highly polished hammer and anvil. He placed the
item on the anvil and gently tapped out any flaws or
hammer marks left on its surface by previous pro-
cedures.

Drawing out lengthened or widened a piece of
metal or its ends. It could be done on an anvil using a

hammer. It was also done by pulling metal through an opening between two drawing irons usually held together by a vise. There were hundreds of uses for drawing out. Each smith used it in different ways. Wire, horseshoes, and ornamental rims and bottoms for teapots are some examples of drawn items.

Small sections of an item, such as a rim, were seamed to larger ones using solder. Solder is a molten form of a metal or its alloy, occasionally used with a fluxing agent. Solder always has a lower melting point than the metal it is being used to hold together.

Decorating processes included engraving, chasing, and repoussé. Engraving is accomplished by using gravers and hammers to cut a design into the surface of an item. Chasing is making an impression of a design on the surface of the work. Repoussé is done by hammering a design from the back or inside of the work. This results in a raised design on the surface of a piece. In order to produce both chasing and repoussé, punches were struck with hammers.

Finally, all colonial smiths could cast metal objects. The procedure was frequently begun by cutting a pattern from wood. The pattern was placed in a flask and dampened sand was rammed around it. Sand was used for several reasons. It was porous and easily released the gases of the cooling metal. Sand was able to pick up any intricate detailing in the pattern. And sand molds were cheap to make. After removing the pattern, the smith filled the form it left with molten metal. When the metal was cool, the sand was knocked away and the finished piece was removed from the cast. Cast-iron molds were also used. However, they cost a lot, and styles changed quickly. It was much wiser for colonial smiths to use inexpensive, versatile sand molds.

Smiths have hammered, cast, and molded metals in countless ways for thousands of years. Colonial metalworkers did the same as they forged their place in history.

SILVERSMITHS AND GOLDSMITHS

Modern American cities are full of banks and jewelry stores. Phrases like, "You can take that to the bank," and "You can bank on it," mean you can depend on something. The early colonists didn't coin these phrases. They had no banks. They depended on goldsmiths and silversmiths to turn their wealth into tangible products.

By the late seventeenth century, colonial businesses had grown and the economy had prospered. People wanted to invest in something they knew would keep its value. No one trusted paper money—it could be counterfeited. Silver coins could be stolen and never recovered. But silverplate was marked. It was easily identified by the owner as well as the silversmith who made it.

In addition to making silver plate, early American goldsmiths and silversmiths made jewelry and clocks. Some also doubled as dentists since they knew how to work with silver and gold. This angered *real* colonial dentists. They felt superior to "those smiths" because, as dentists, they had some medical training. Silversmiths, in turn, resented blacksmiths who worked with gold and silver. They felt blacksmiths were too uncouth to work with precious metals. However, there was no jealousy between goldsmiths and silversmiths. Sometimes artisans who worked only with silver even called themselves goldsmiths because of the status connected with gold.

Until silver was discovered in the United States, silversmiths relied on three sources for their raw material. Customers brought them old silver plate to be

A seventeenth-century engraving shows
many of the tools and techniques used
by colonial silversmiths, including
a tree stump anvil in the foreground.

melted down and reworked into newer styles. Some
silver came from the mines of Peru and Mexico. The
third, and most interesting source, was pirates' booty.

Although pirates were outlaws, their activities were
often ignored in the large cities of the north. British
coins, which contained a lot of silver, were in limited
supply in the colonies. A desperate silversmith
wouldn't hesitate to deal with a poor sailor who
brought him a treasure of foreign coins. The craftsperson didn't question where the sailor got them. He

only cared about the silver that remained after he melted the coins and removed all of the impurities. Silver by itself is too soft to shape into objects, so it is alloyed with copper to strengthen it. Sterling silver is 925 parts silver and 75 parts copper.

The colonial silversmith was pleased when a customer brought him old silver articles. English pieces were highly prized because of their purity. They were engraved with four marks required by the Worshipful Company of Goldsmiths of the City of London—the British lion passant or the figure of Britannia, the maker's mark, the assay date, and a hallmark—which certified that the piece was 92.5 percent silver. These marks showed the piece had been appraised according to the guild's standards. English silversmiths could not sell their silver plate until it had been assayed.

Colonial silversmiths had neither assay offices nor standards to govern their work. Their customers had to rely on the honesty of the craftsperson. Each artisan personally guaranteed that he produced silver of "sterling quality." Unfortunately, this was not always true. Many early American pieces appraised in modern times do not meet sterling standards. Whether or not certain colonial silversmiths did this intentionally cannot be determined.

Master colonial silversmiths had one strong tie with their English counterparts. They were adamant that their apprentices would receive no less than seven years' training. The young servant would usually start his workday by lighting a fire in the forge. He also delivered the products finished the day before. Perhaps the boy had the unhappy task of acting as his master's bill collector. When he had a difficult time accomplishing this task, the apprentice could soothe his master's feelings by bringing him cakes and ale. For a few moments, the two enjoyed the colonial equivalent of today's coffee break.

The apprentice also assisted in refining the silver. After weighing an item in front of its owner, the master placed it into a black lead or graphite crucible. The master lowered the crucible into the fire. Charcoal was placed on top of the melting silver to prevent it from absorbing too much oxygen. Now the apprentice took over. For the next fifteen to twenty minutes, he kept the bellows in constant motion, which kept the fire hot enough to melt the silver.

As the silver melted, most of the impurities in it were absorbed by the porous material of the crucible. The molten silver was poured into a two-piece cast-iron ingot mold, or into an open mold called a skillet. After the silver cooled and hardened, the ingot, or bar of silver, was stored until the silversmith was ready to shape it.

The basic shaping techniques frequently used by silversmiths were hammering, casting, and seaming or building. The bodies of the products were often forged by raising.

To raise silver, the master had to do more than beat an ingot with all his might. Everything was planned. First he made a detailed drawing of the item he wanted to create. Next he forged an ingot into a flat plate. Using calipers, the silversmith measured his drawing. He carefully cut a disk from the plate, according to the drawing's measurements. Using a compass, he marked a series of circles from the center of the disk to its edge.

It might be hard to believe, but the artisan might have laid the disk on top of a huge tree stump. Although most anvils were made from iron, tree stumps also were used as anvils by many silversmiths. They were hard, yet absorbed the shock of the hammer's blows. Hollows of different diameters and depths were first formed in the wood. The smith placed the disk over the hollow he wanted. Following the pattern of drawn circles, he hit the metal with a hollowing ham-

Native American silversmiths, using only
simple equipment, created metal products
of high technical standards and beauty.

mer. He started at the center of the disk and worked
toward the edge. As he worked, the craftsman an-
nealed brittle silver using an acid bath called pickle.
The hammering continued until the disk became a flat-
bottomed piece with flared sides. It could now be
shaped into any type of hollowware.

Additional shaping was done on a stake using a raising hammer. The artisan struck the metal on the outside with even blows. This caused the silver to mold around the projection of the small anvil.

After the body of the item was formed, it was planished. Masters were extremely fussy about their planishing hammers and anvils. Flaws in either one would be transferred to the product's surface. If his tools weren't perfect, the artisan would refinish them. He stored them in tallow to prevent them from tarnishing and rusting. When planishing was completed, smaller parts could be seamed to the body of the piece.

Usually parts like lids, finials, and spouts were made by casting. They then were attached to the body with solder made of bits of silver and an alloy. The solder was placed on the seam with a little borax. The pieces were wired together. Then the silversmith carefully melted the solder with a blowpipe. After all the pieces were seamed, the item could be decorated. The article was then given its last polishing.

Rottenstone, a soft rock; pumice, a soft volcanic ash; tripoli, decomposed limestone; and jeweler's rouge were all used to create silver's characteristic luster.

Finally, the silversmith would "strike his mark" on the piece, identifying himself as its maker.

Not every item a silversmith made had his mark on it. Mourning rings were very fashionable and could be made "on the shortest of notice." They were worn by the relatives and friends of a deceased person. Usually a man provided money in his will for these black enamel rings.

Silversmiths and goldsmiths were able to make fashionable jewelry using a technique known as inlaying. Depressions were made in the surface of the gold. Then precious or semiprecious stones, mother of pearl, or smaller pieces of silver and gold were soldered into place. Filigree was a design made by soldering beads or grains of gold, silver, and sometimes copper, onto larger pieces.

Damascening, another type of engraving, entailed cutting a dovetail design on the back of an item. Silver or gold wire was placed into the design. Then the wire was beaten, which caused it to swell up and become permanently attached to the piece.

Goldsmiths are responsible for one of the oldest crafts that still cannot be duplicated by machines. It is called gold beating.

Because it is the most ductile metal, gold can be hammered into sheets measuring only 0.000004 of an inch in thickness. Skilled gold beaters can beat a three-inch cube of gold so thin, it will cover one acre of ground. In the colonies, these paper-thin sheets, called gold leaf, were used to trim books.

Clock making was a sideline craft for goldsmiths. Making a clock involved only a few tools—a hammer, a file, and a drill. But it also took technical knowledge and a lot of time. Some colonial clocks had wooden gears because brass was hard to get, but when it was available, the goldsmith cast brass plates for gears. He filed and polished the gears. They were assembled with springs made by the goldsmith to complete the clock's mechanism. Eventually, brass blanks were cast between two polished slabs of marble. Even later, the goldsmith could buy readymade brass castings and blanks that only had to be filed and assembled.

Early clocks were expensive. They were called "wag-on-the-wall" and were not encased. Clock makers began to realize that oiling and cleaning clocks' gears made them run better and last longer. Cabinetmakers and glaziers also benefitted from this discovery when it became practical—and fashionable—to enclose clocks in wooden cabinets with glass faces.

Silversmiths and goldsmiths can be considered America's first bankers. They turned colonists' savings

An eighteenth-century engraving shows
craftsworkers in a goldsmith's shop.

into marketable items that maintained value. They created stunning jewelry and kept more than one colonist
on time for appointments. One particular colonial silversmith was also an excellent horseman.

Paul Revere's famous midnight ride and shouts of, "To arms, the British are coming," will live forever in American history.

WHITESMITHS

It is said that tin is a poor man's silver. If this is so, a whitesmith was a poor man's silversmith.

Tin was in short supply in the early colonies. When it was available, the whitesmith worked *exactly* as did a silversmith or a goldsmith. He too needed a knowledge of geometry to design and develop his products. And he was an expert at drawing out because he made thousands of yards of wire. The most notable difference in his technique was the way he seamed. The whitesmith would overlay or fold the edges of his products before he seamed them.

Whitesmiths used a beautiful finishing process called japanning. First the article was scoured with sandstone. It was painted with a special black varnish and baked in an oven for ten to twelve hours until it hardened. Extra coats of varnish were applied and hardened. Then the whitesmith added gold or bronze bands to the piece. He next painted or transferred floral designs or scenes onto the shiny black finish. Finally, the piece was hardened one last time.

Lacquering was another finishing process. It was used to put color or transparent varnishes on metals to protect them. Lacquering could give tin the appearance of other metals. For example, a lacquer was applied to tin to make it look like gold.

The article to be lacquered was pickled in a blend of water and an acid called aquafortis for six to eight hours. This cleaned the grease and dirt from it. The piece was gently heated. Lacquer was spread over it, and then it was dried. No further work was necessary.

Tin articles that were not protected could actually develop a "disease" called tin plague. At 14 degrees Fahrenheit, tin infected with the plague would disintegrate into a pile of powder. This could really shock an unsuspecting apprentice. Only one thing might surprise him more—"tin cry."

Tin cry is a creaking sound tin makes when the metal is bent and its crystals change their positions. If an apprentice was alone in his master's shop and exposed to both of these phenomena at once, he probably ran screaming from the shop, never to be seen again!

THE IRONWORKERS

Foghorns moaning in the distance, chains dragging across the floor, groans and labored breathing, heavy objects crashing to the ground . . .

These sounds could be the chilling sound track of a suspenseful movie. They could also be sounds an apprentice heard daily as he sweated in a shipsmith's shop.

Shipsmiths, blacksmiths, cutlers, and farriers were all craftspeople who forged iron into useful products. A shipsmith made nautical items like cleats, harpoons, anchors, and chains. A blacksmith produced pots and pans, hardware, wheel parts, and more. The cutler's specialties included all types of knives and swords, scissors, and surgical instruments. The farrier spent his time shoeing horses and oxen. Many blacksmiths and farriers also advertised their veterinary skills.

BLACKSMITHS

Blacksmiths claim, "For by Hammer and Hand all arts do stand." It's not an empty boast. No other colonial trades could develop until the blacksmith established his business. He made and repaired the tools of all other craftspeople. In the early colonies, he was usually the only person who knew anything about repairing guns. He made the axes that felled the trees to build houses. No other smith was more necessary to the colonists' survival than the blacksmith.

When the Virginia Company formed, one of its main objectives was to establish an iron industry in Virginia. England's supply of iron was running low. It was relying on iron imported from Scandinavian countries. The first full-scale American ironworks was operating in 1620 at Falling Creek, a settlement about eighty miles north of Jamestown. Its success was short-lived. In 1622, Indians massacred most of the workers at the ironworks and destroyed the buildings and equipment.

After the massacre, finances became a problem for the owners of the Virginia Company. Instead of re-establishing the ironworks, they built a bloomery.

A bloomery was a simple establishment for producing wrought iron. It had a plain open hearth with a bellows and a fire bed filled with charcoal. Pieces of iron ore were placed on the charcoal to soften. The fire was intensified by blasts from the bellows. Impurities were drawn out of the ore as slag. Liquid iron particles fused and absorbed carbon. Spongy masses of iron, known as blooms, were produced. The blooms were heated and pounded with heavy hammers several times. This process removed any remaining impurities and reduced the iron's carbon content. Finally, refined wrought iron was pounded into bars for storage; this was called bar iron.

Although colonists were now producing some iron, the Virginia Company still had problems. Apprentices and hard cash were rare in the infant colonies. There were no stores where people could buy food and supplies. Incentives were offered to get craftspeople, especially ironworkers, to come to America. Land was

An early colonial method of producing iron

cheap, and the artisans who came purchased huge tracts of it, particularly along navigable waterways. But when they discovered they could become rich growing tobacco and other crops, they gave up their crafts. Their plantations became self-contained. They built docks so English ships could pick up tobacco and drop off English products. Each plantation usually had its own blacksmith, tanner, carpenter, and mill. The owners relied on each other for entertainment and socializing. There was little to encourage craftspeople to return to their trades.

The Virginia legislature took action. It stopped the importation of iron and other commodities useful to craftspeople. If artisans gave up farming and returned

Gunsmiths in Pennsylvania produced an
extremely accurate long rifle often called the Kentucky
rifle, which became famous in that colony.

to their trades, they didn't have to pay taxes or levies.
But even this didn't help the situation. Finally, the legislature had to pass a law making it mandatory for all
blacksmiths to become armorers in order to repair
guns and other weaponry, and maintain the local militia's guns. The safety of the colonists might depend on
the condition of their weapons. If a craftsperson refused to do this, he could be heavily fined.

As the seventeenth century closed, there were enough people in the colonies to keep blacksmiths steadily employed in some towns. People needed wagons, mills, equipment for small farms, nails, and more. America's iron industry began to flourish. The colonies' dependency on English iron products decreased.

The English became resentful. To stop the growth of America's iron industry and to encourage Americans to export bar iron to England, Parliament passed the Iron Act of 1750. It had little effect on the colonists. They continued producing iron, especially in Pennsylvania. There, deposits of iron ore and coal were mined by German settlers long known as expert miners and ironworkers.

Coal, free of sulfur and phosphorus, was the fuel ironworkers preferred to use. Charcoal was used, but it was not always suitable for all smithy operations. It was lighter than coal and could be blown around the fire bed by powerful blasts from the bellows. When his fire's hot spot was destroyed, only the blacksmith's temper flared.

Colonial blacksmiths took their work seriously. Silversmiths probably snubbed them as barbarians because they "upset" iron and used "snarling" tools. The joke was on the silversmiths. Upsetting was the opposite of drawing. This process was used for compressing and thickening iron. Snarling tools were used for rounding out vessels. Blacksmiths also used drawing, welding, and punching techniques to shape iron. Other tools frequently used were swages, punches, and wrenches. No other tools were used more often than hammers, tongs, and anvils.

Anvils used by ironworkers could weigh over five hundred pounds. If an anvil had a rounded heel and a pointed horn, they were used for bending iron into numerous shapes. The anvil's hard face was kept smooth and flat. It was where the heavy pounding was done. A small square area between the face and the horn, called the table, was used as a cutting surface. It was softer than the face and wouldn't damage cutting tools when they hit it. There were two holes in the anvil. The round "pritchel" hole held tools with round shanks. It was also used when the ironworker punched holes in an item. The "hardie" hole was larger and square. It held auxiliary anvils and "hardies," square-shanked chisels.

Pieces of metal separately forged on anvils could be joined by welding. Apprentices learned to properly heat these pieces and keep them free of dirt. They also learned that the hotter iron gets, the more oxygen it absorbs. This oxidation causes scaling in the metal. Apprentices knew if the metal was dirty or full of scale, no amount of hammering would weld it together. To prevent scale or dissolve it, a fluxing agent was wiped on the metal prior to heating it. The flux was forced out of the welding joint when it was hammered.

When welding, the blacksmith would first upset the joint area in case accidental drawing occurred when the iron was hammered. The pieces to be welded were heated to a brilliant white. They sparkled and hissed when exposed to the air. Pieces heated to this temperature became pasty and would stick together when they touched. The smith joined them with pressure or one heavy hammer blow. If the pieces didn't weld, they were returned to the fire for additional heating.

After the pieces were joined, the blacksmith continued hammering. This broke up crystals that were formed by the high heat of the fire. It also gave the iron a strong grain and created a weld that was almost as strong as bar iron.

Iron work too thin to be welded would be brazed. The pieces would be joined by means of a brass or silver solder. Sometimes blacksmiths referred to brazing as welding.

Although blacksmiths were originally jacks-of-all-trades, their craft became specialized as the need for their services increased.

FARRIERS

Colonial farriers were men with iron nerves. Their customers would frequently bite, kick, and step on them. Since each of their customers weighed twelve hundred to twenty-five hundred pounds, a farrier could be seriously injured. Farriers shoed horses and oxen. They also recognized and treated many ailments these animals experienced.

The farrier began his task by removing the animal's old shoes. He trimmed dead and ragged tissue from the soles of its feet. The hooves were filed to a proper angle. Then each foot was measured. The iron shoes were shaped using a hammer, the face and horn of an anvil, tongs, and the forging techniques of drawing and upsetting. The farrier welded a clip to the top side of the shoe. The clip prevented the animal's foot from slipping and helped the shoe fit securely. The farrier placed each shoe over the pritchel hole in his anvil and used a punch to make holes for the nails. The nails were beveled and tapered to ensure that they would enter the hoof at the proper angle. Even though horses and oxen have no feeling in their hooves, the farrier used caution when nailing the shoes onto them. If the nail went into the flesh of the foot, it would be extremely painful. The animal would react with a well-placed bite or kick to the farrier. The sharp tips of the nails came out the side of the hooves. They were removed and the blunt ends that remained were bent down. The hooves and shoes were filed one last time to make them even. In most cases, the farrier and horse parted friends.

Shoeing horses was easy compared to shoeing oxen. Their shoes were made in two parts because they have small cloven feet. It was also impossible for a heavy ox

The farrier changing a horse's shoe often
attracted an audience of colonial children.

to stand on three feet while having the fourth one
shoed. To solve this problem, the colonial farrier
hoisted the animal off the ground in a special sling.
The farrier got the job done, but usually traumatized
the ox. This craftsperson loved animals ... but the
feeling wasn't always mutual.

CUTLERS

Boys who were apprenticed to cutlers had to be sharp students. They learned to shape iron and steel into instruments that saved lives or weapons that took them. They also became experts in making and repairing tools with cutting edges.

Cutting tools were made by combining steel cutting edges with iron in a process called steeling. Steel was made by allowing the carbon absorbed during smelting to remain in the iron. When someone needed a cutting tool repaired, the cutler would lay, or resteel, it.

The steel for the cutting edge was placed between pieces of iron that would become the tool's head. The metals were welded until they were fused and the head was properly shaped. Tools made this way were stronger than tools made solely of steel.

After the tool's head was welded, the edge was hardened. There were two ways to do this. The cutler could heat the edge to a blood-red and then plunge it into cold water. Saws and straight rulers are examples of products hardened in this manner. The second method, hammer-hardening, was done by hammering the metal smooth. Then it was beaten back into its own body. Scissors, shears, springs, and punches are some items that were hammer-hardened.

All hardened cutting edges were tempered for lasting wear. If they weren't, they would become brittle and crumble or break when used.

To temper a cutting edge, the cutler scraped any black scale from the blade with a whetstone. This brightened the blade. He heated to a light gold color items like files, cold chisels, and punches used for punching iron and steel. Punches used on brass and most sharp-edged tools were heated to a dark gold. Then the metal was allowed to cool slowly and naturally. A wooden handle was inserted into the head, and the tool was finished.

Any cutting tool or weapon could be made using the same processes. Hilts for swords and daggers, made by any metalworker or woodworker, could be quite decorative. The metal parts of better-quality weapons could even be "gilded," or covered with a precious metal like gold.

Before there was enough work to keep a cutler occupied, all colonial ironworkers were able to produce fine cutting tools, swords, daggers, and bayonets.

FOUNDERS

A founder was a craftsperson who made metal castings, usually for other artisans. Iron foundries developed as the increasing colonial population brought an increasing need for bells, cannons, and other large items made from iron, and as more metalworkers came to the colonies.

The techniques of the founders were generally the same regardless of the metal used or the size of their castings. Most foundry work was done in three steps.

The patternmaker made the wooden patterns to be used in the molds. He was often a carpenter or a joiner. His patterns were oversized because metal shrinks as it cools. The patternmaker's skill included a knowledge of how much each metal would shrink. He gauged the size of his patterns based on this knowledge.

The molder used the patterns to make sand molds. He made certain there was a "sprue" in each mold. The sprue was a funnel-shaped hole used for pouring molten metal into the mold. Several smaller holes, called risers, were also made in the mold. These holes allowed gases from the cooling metal to escape. The holes were made by inserting tapered tubes into the wet sand. The sand would fill the tubes. When the tubes were removed from the mold, the holes were left behind.

The founder was the person who poured the metal

and cleaned the casting. His job was not easy. The metal had to be correctly mixed. Its temperature had to be just right. When pouring, the founder had to make the stream exactly right for the sprue. All impurities had to be skimmed off the surface of the molten metal so they didn't enter the casting. The founder had to be careful not to allow the metal to burst out of the mold during the pouring. If he were casting a cannon, this craftsperson had to be absolutely positive that no air entered the metal in the casting. If it did, the cannon would explode when it was fired.

CUTTERS OF PUNCHES AND DIES

The cutter of punches and dies was no chiseler when it came to his craft. He used all of his talent to change pieces of metal into art.

This artisan could run a mint and make coins without any help. He created embossed stamps. They were used to impress official seals on documents such as deeds. People also used them to seal envelopes. Intaglio, engraved printing, also referred to as steel-die printing, was done using dies the cutter made. Bank notes were printed using intaglio dies. Wafer irons used to make hosts for the Eucharist came from the cutter's shop. The cutter's most important contribution to the colonies was the metal type he created for the printer. He had to cut everything in reverse, but the work produced using his dies and punches read properly.

The cutter used chisels, files, drills, and punched dies, along with hammers and anvils. To make coins, two dies were used. An anvil die had the coin's face cut into it. A punch die was the coin's tail, or reverse, side.

Coins started as blanks. Blanks were made from blobs of metal, or by casting. Each one was weighed to make sure it met the official standard.

The cutter placed a heated blank on the anvil die.

He put the punch die on top of the blank. Then he pounded the dies with a heavy hammer. Both sides of the coin were impressed at the same time.

Dies made for embossed stamps also had two parts. Each part had an identical design carved into it. The paper to be embossed was placed between the two dies, and they were squeezed together. Modern notary stamps work on a similar principle.

Type was designed by the cutter. Each type punch was cut in reverse and hardened. The face of the punch was driven into a piece of bronze or copper. The resulting indentation was called a matrix. The matrix was fitted into a two-part mold, and metal was poured into it. The mold was shaken. This drove the melted metal into the matrix. The mold was opened and the new type was removed. A complete font included one matrix for each capital letter, small capital letter, lowercase letter, punctuation mark, and numeral.

PEWTERERS

Pewterers can be classified as founders rather than smiths because of the techniques used in their craft.

There were only a few pewterers in the very early colonies. Their work consisted of repairing or reworking English pieces. It was difficult to get the materials to make pewter. Fine pewter was 90 percent tin. Copper, antimony, or bismuth were used as hardeners. Pewter also contained about 5 percent lead. This small amount of lead made the alloy easier to cast and work. Very low quality pewter contained as much as 40 percent lead because it was cheaper than tin. This amount of lead could be poisonous. Usually only articles like bedpans were made of low quality pewter.

Pewterware was cast. After it was removed from the mold, any pits were filled with scraps of pewter. The surface was smoothed with a two-handled float. This tool resembled a file with a course horizontal cutting ridge. The item was then skimmed on a treadle or great wheel lathe. During skimming, the pewterer pulled a hook or other type of cutting or scraping tool across the article. A round, polished burnisher dipped in soap suds followed the hook to flatten the marks of the skimming process. The item was polished with rottenstone and a leather pad. Any seams were fluxed with rosin. Another light skimming made the seams invisible.

Sometimes slush molds were used for making hollow handles for tankards or nursing bottles. The mold was shaped like the outside of the article. Hot pewter was poured into the cast. It was carefully swirled around. The artisan poured out any extra metal, but enough stuck to the inside of the mold to form a hollow vessel.

Pewter was easily bent. A piece used often required frequent straightening by hand. Eventually, the metal broke and the piece was set aside until the tinker arrived to fix it.

TINKER

The tinker was the one metalworker who was not considered a craftsperson. He traveled around offering to repair broken metal products. He particularly enjoyed working on copper and tin articles. Sometimes his work was properly done. More often, it was shoddy and of poor quality.

The majority of tinkers were of questionable character. When a repair job fell apart, the customer couldn't complain to the tinker. He was usually gone, along with the customer's money.

As customers tossed the useless articles aside, they

Glassmakers arrived in Jamestown in 1608,
but glassmaking did not become a real industry
in the colonies until 1739, when Caspar Wistar
established a factory in Salem County,
New Jersey. Here a master glassblower, called
a gaffer, blows a bubble of glass to the size he
needs. The glass is pliable at this point and
can be stretched, twisted, or flattened into
any shape. An apprentice, or a worker called
the fireman, makes sure the fire stays hot.

remarked, "That's not worth a tinker's damn." The phrase referred to anything worthless, and the tinker's tendency to use profanity.

As long as demands for particular items could keep metalworkers in business, they continued to branch out. Their names and products became specialized. However, their techniques and tools rarely changed. These craftspeople shaped metals using the methods of their ancestors. Their constant willingness to learn and adapt helped them to forge toward the Industrial Revolution of the nineteenth century.

CHAPTER SIX

Fashion Comes to the Colonies

"Can you believe she's wearing *that!*"

"Honestly, she's *never* in style."

"Oh, not me! *I'd* rather be *dead* than unfashionable."

Comments like these are not unique to modern times. For centuries people have used fashion to reflect their social status. The colonists were no different. They flaunted their wealth through material possessions and fine clothing. Idealistic American founders wrote, "All men are created equal." Yet a woman dressed in coarse linen was treated very differently from one who wore silk and satin.

MILLINER

Colonial women depended on the milliner for fashion advice. The original meaning of the word milliner has never been agreed upon. In the colonies, it was the woman who sold a "thousand different wares" to ladies to "set off their Beauty, increase their Vanity, or render them ridiculous."[1]

There were no women in the original Jamestown settlement. And only twenty-eight women and children arrived on the *Mayflower*. Few of them survived the first winter in America. By 1625, male colonists were desperate for wives to run their homes. They also wanted children. Single women who came to the colonies didn't remain single for long. Female indentured servants frequently married the men who bought their contracts. Lonely women were thrilled to marry pompous men. Romantic love was rarely involved in these marriages of convenience. Prestige and social status were far more important.

The eighteenth century is considered by some to be an elegant era. Others view it as a shallow one. Girls were taught that their primary goal in life was to marry well. They constantly worried about their appearance.

It was more important for a young woman to master social and sewing skills than academics. It was considered an achievement if a girl could sew tiny, neat stitches. Even after there were plenty of dressmakers and milliners in the colonies, colonial women spent hours with a needle and thread. Sewing also was an important social pastime. Women took their needlework with them when they visited their friends. Sometimes one woman read a novel aloud while the others sewed. Women proudly displayed and admired impressively decorated needlecases, pincushions, and work

A fashionable couple of the late
seventeenth century

baskets brought to these gatherings. They also used these opportunities to spread the latest gossip.

Because such an emphasis was placed on sewing, it was only natural that many women of "unfortunate circumstances" would become dressmakers. Unfortunate circumstances meant that a woman was a widow who had no other means of support, or she was single. Women who ventured into the business world faced different obstacles than their male counterparts.

In the colonies, single women could enter into contracts; manage estates; sue or be sued; and own, buy, or sell property. But when they got married, their husbands took over management of their businesses, property, and earnings. Unless a woman had an "antenuptial contract," which allowed her to keep control of her affairs, she could lose everything. Her

The craft of bobbin lacemaking was worked on
a pillow with bobbins. The craft required great
dexterity and produced beautiful, intricate lace
pieces. (A sample is shown.) Since small
hands were helpful in this work, girls as
young as four were taught the craft.

husband could squander everything she had ever acquired, and she had no legal grounds to fight him.

Official records show that girls were apprenticed to milliners. They used reading and arithmetic to order goods and keep accurate records. Any dressmaking skills they had were enhanced as they learned to design clothing.

Milliners had unique problems when hiring apprentices or journeywomen. Newspaper articles were written warning parents not to bond their daughters to milliners. These pieces stated that frivolous "beaus and rakes" would "trifle with the affections" of innocent young women who worked for milliners. The writers claimed that daughters would be "spoiled" so that no honest man would want them. Others hinted that millinery shops were fronts for serious misconduct.

Frequently young women in need of employment simply advertised their sewing services. When they received a job, their salaries included room and board. They lived in their employer's home until the sewing was completed. Accepting work like this enabled a woman to save enough money to open her own shop.

A dressmaker's shop was often started in the front room of her home. She added to her income by selling sewing supplies to other women. Within time, her shop could cover several floors of a building. Large shops kept several full-time needleworkers employed and sold everything from hats, ribbons, and jewelry to stationery items and pills. It was sometimes difficult to tell the difference between a millinery shop and a general store.

Some women who opened millinery shops were just merchants. Others increased their income by taking in boarders or selling lottery tickets.

Like male craftspeople, dressmakers and milliners had to be adaptable in order to earn money. The two trades rarely competed. The dressmaker, sometimes called a mantua-maker, sold a greater variety of gar-

In addition to visiting milliners and
dressmakers, a colonial woman could
also order a new garment from a tailor.

ments than the milliner. She usually sold only clothing made in her shop. The milliner sold ready-made articles as well as her own creations. The competition among women following the *same* trade could be interesting.

Unlike other trades, business went to the dressmaker and milliner who had the very latest in fashion. The milliner made trips to England to buy goods for her shop and to study fashion trends. When this wasn't possible, she hired an agent to stay in Europe. These agents used all the tactics of spies to prevent the hottest information from falling into the hands of the competition. The milliner's agent had to be completely loyal.

The agent also supplied information about current European headgear. A stylish colonial woman had numerous cloth caps, bonnets, hoods, and at least one straw hat. The milliner sold them all. She reshaped old straw hats into the latest styles using steam. Then she added or removed accessories like feathers, ribbons, or lace. She also sold all the popular accessories so women could fashion their own hats. Colonial women could have the same straw hat for thirty years, but it always looked different. The milliner even sold a variety of men's items including knitted caps and ready-made hats. The men's hats were made by hatmakers.

HATMAKERS

Colonial women weren't the only ones interested in their appearance. Colonial men were obsessed by hats and wigs. They didn't go anywhere without a hat. Even when a man wore a wig, he carried his tricornered hat under his arm. If a man got caught in the rain, the brim of his hat would lose its shape and have to be reblocked. Sometimes a man couldn't afford to have this done. He'd continue to wear the hat. It was better to have a floppy brimmed hat than none at all.

It's hard to believe, but pelts from beaver, otter, seal, muskrat, and rabbit could be made into hats by simply being cut, matted, squashed, kneaded, layered, boiled, rolled, battered, molded, baked, shaved, smoothed, ironed, and paddled.

The hatmaker made most of his hats from felt, however. This material was made by matting wool or the undercoat of animal pelts. First the fur was washed, combed, and weighed into piles. Each pile would become a hat. The fur was placed onto a hurl, which was a table enclosed on three sides. Suspended from the ceiling was a giant rectangular strung bow. As he passed the bow through the fur, the hatmaker plucked the sheepgut string of the bow with a knobbed bowpin. The vibration of the string crossing the hairs caused them to cling together.

The bowed hairs were patted into round-topped pyramids. These pyramids were squashed with a slatted wooden hatter's basket. The well-matted, flattened hairs were called a batt.

Batts, separated by wet linen towels, were stacked on top of each other. A second craftsperson kneaded pairs of these batts. The kneading formed the batt into a cone-shaped hood that would become the hat's body. The hoods were boiled for six to eight hours. This fulling process caused the hoods to shrink and thicken. Next the hoods were sent to the battery.

The battery was a kettle in a brick enclosure. A sloping wooden plank was built around the top of the bricks. The kettle contained a mild acid solution that was kept boiling. The hoods were repeatedly dipped into the kettle, then rolled and planked. Planking was done by beating the hood with a club. During this procedure knotted hairs and impurities were removed from the hood. If needed, more fur was patted onto the body with a wet brush.

After all this work, the only thing the hatter had

In a hatmaker's shop, craftspeople work on
hoods at the battery. In the back room, the
master works at the hurl, creating batts.

was a soaking wet hood that was half its original size. It
then had to be blocked to shape it.

Blocks were molds of different sizes and shapes.
Each one was attached to a circular bottom board. This
board represented the brim of the hat, the block was
the crown.

The master slapped the soppy hood onto the block. Using a runner-down stick, he stretched it over the block. He flattened the brim onto the board and removed any wrinkles from it. The shaped hat was popped into a slightly warmed oven. It was dried overnight with the rest of the hats made that day. The hats were removed in the morning by the finisher.

The finisher trimmed each hat's brim. The surfaces were smoothed with a pumice stone. The finisher ironed the hats and paddled them, not because they were bad, but in order to raise the nap. He shaved off any wild hairs that refused to lay properly and brushed the nap in one direction. A leather headband was stitched to the inside. Decorations like crown ribbons and edge bindings were added. Brims that were to be cocked were steamed, rolled upward, and taped while the hat dried on a block.

As with all crafts, the hatter varied his technique according to the fur or wool he was using. Wool hats had glue or varnish added during the felting process. Cheap hats were rolled in cloth during planking so they wouldn't fall apart.

After a final brushing, the hatmaker's apprentice carried some of his master's products to the milliner. Others were left behind to be sold directly by the hatmaker.

The colonial hatmakers did an excellent job. As the trade developed, their hats were sold locally and exported to other countries. When exports reached about 10,000 hats, English hatmakers screamed. Once again, Parliament tried to stop American initiative with the Hat Act of 1731. It banned the exportation of colonial hats. It forbade blacks to learn the trade. It limited to two the number of apprentices each master hatmaker could have. These boys had to complete a full seven years in bondage. But it did not stop the colonists. They simply shifted their attention to other areas. Production of cheaper woolen hats and other fabrics increased. Many were sold to plantation owners to be worn by their slaves.

American beavers sighed with relief as the eighteenth century drew to a close. When silk hats appeared in 1831, it was the silk worms, not the beavers, who met the demand for raw material.

WIGMAKERS

Modern men do everything they can to prevent hair loss or to hide the fact that they are bald. Colonial men paid to have someone shave their heads and keep them bald. Wigs fit so much better when one's natural hair was gone.

Thanks to France's King Louis XIII, and other monarchs, wigs were all the rage in the seventeenth and eighteenth centuries. It seems the young French king was going bald at twenty-three. He became depressed and put on a wig. All of his courtiers jumped on the bandwagon. After all, in order to stay in his good graces, anything the king did, you did too. Women adorned their wigs with jewels and fresh flowers. Some wigs were so ridiculously high, women actually hid vases of water in them to keep the flowers alive.

Elizabeth I, who was queen of England from 1558–1603, had an entire wardrobe of wigs. Mary, Queen of Scots, wore a wig to her beheading. King Charles II wasn't happy with his graying hair, so he put on a wig. Soon all English aristocrats were wearing large wigs. Today the term, "bigwig," still refers to someone who has power or prominence.

There was controversy in the colonies about wigs. Some puritan preachers yelled and screamed from the pulpit that they were evil. Other religious leaders felt they were an innocent fashion.

Wigmakers flocked to America. They were kept busy making new wigs, and maintaining old wigs was big business, too.

European wigs were quite colorful in the truest sense. They came in natural hair colors, as well as blue and pink! Colonists were a bit more reserved. They stayed with the natural hair colors, although there was a preference for white powdered wigs.

Before a wig could be worn, the person's natural hair (if there was any) was greased. A hand bellows resembling a fat elephant's trunk was used to apply the powder to the wig. The person's face was well covered with a mask specifically designed for this purpose.

Wigs came in a variety of styles. Colonists wore wigs that reflected their professional or social status. The "great" or "full-bottomed" wig was very aristocratic. Masses of curls framed the wearer's face as others fell over his shoulders and chest. By the early eighteenth century, this style became a little more reserved. Also, beginning about 1700, wigs with pigtails called queues became popular to control the volume of hair. The tie wig had curls tied with a black bow at the nape of the neck. The pigtail wig had black ribbon interlaced in its queue. Another favorite, the bagwig, had a black bag with a drawstring covering the pigtail. A large black bow was tied at its top.

By 1750, professional men replaced the great wig with the physical wig that resembled a long bob. Craftspeople usually wore the major bob. It had several rows of close-fitting curls surrounding the head. The lower half of the man's ears were left exposed. Apprentices and poor people wore the minor bob. This was also a shorter wig, but straight, not curly.

Even the military got into wigs. The famous Ramillies wig, named after the Battle of Ramillies, was the soldiers' favorite. It had one queue tied at the top and the bottom with black ribbons.

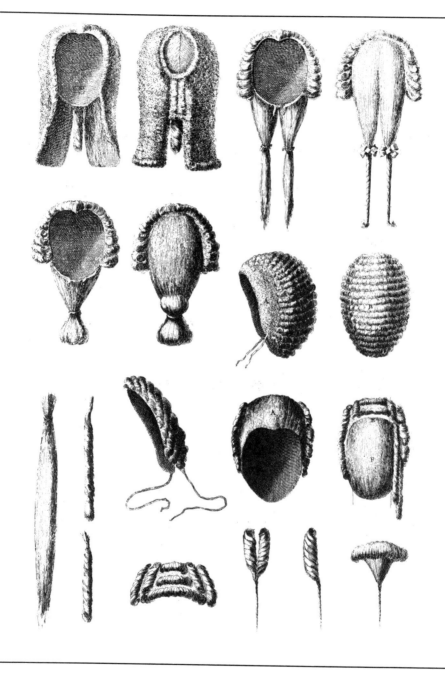

Spiking hair is not new. One popular wig, the hedgehog, had its top and side brushed out into spikes. The hair was about two to three inches in length. Women wore a modified hedgehog. Their wigs had extra hair combed into curls on the side.

After deciding what style wig he wanted, the customer had his head shaved. Then it was measured five ways: temple to temple around the back of the head, forehead to nape of neck across the top of the head, ear to ear across the top of the head, from the center of the forehead to each temple, and from each cheek to the back of the head. From these measurements, the wigmaker would make a caul, the net cap or base of the wig. He inserted a drawstring or a buckle so the wig could be tightened.

The customer also had his choice of hair. The wig could be made of anything from human hair to horsehair or cow tails. Even linen and silk threads were used. When all these decisions were made, the wigmaker got to work.

First the chosen hair was cleaned and combed with a fine-toothed hackle. Strands were held in a vise as they were rolled around clay curlers. The curlers were boiled and dried in a small oven. They could be further baked in rye dough at the baker's shop. When they were completely dry, the hair was tested for durability and then trimmed. When he was satisfied with the cleaned and curled hair, the master started to weave it on his weaving frame.

The weaving frame could have three or six silk threads tied between two vertical pegs. Each three

The great variety of styles seen in hair curling and wigs during the eighteenth century

threads represented one side of the wig. The strands of hair were woven up and down and in and around the threads. The woven hairs were fastened in place. This procedure produced fringed layers of hair called weft. The strips of weft were sewn onto the caul a quarter of an inch apart.

When all the weft was in place, the wig was "dressed": curls were rounded, straight hair was combed, ribbons, bags, powder, and perfume might all be added.

The wigmaker was certain to see his customers again and again. Wigs always needed to be freshened. Curls didn't last. Powder and perfume wore off. Men spent hundreds of dollars a year to maintain their headpieces. Women usually dressed their own hair at home. However, in about 1760, when coiffures became too ornate to manage at home, large towns like Philadelphia had hairdressers who catered solely to women. Ladies also needed someone to care for their elaborate wigs. This trend didn't last long. For in the late 1780s, Americans began to abandon wigs in sympathy with the French Revolution.

Perhaps in two hundred years students will giggle at today's hairstyles as we laugh at those of the eighteenth century. But even then, no one will laugh at George Washington. For unlike his contemporaries who sported fancy wigs, Mr. Washington carefully powdered his natural hair.

CHAPTER SEVEN

The Leatherworkers

Colonial tanning had nothing to do with sunbathing. The craftspeople performing this trade didn't enjoy the pleasant fragrance of perfumed oils floating through the air. They smelled only the stench of lime and decaying animal hides and skins. Tanners could honestly say, "My job stinks!"

Colonists may have held their noses around the tanner, but they couldn't deny his importance. They didn't have plastic or rubber during that time. Leather was used for everything from clothing to drumheads. Craftspeople wore leather aprons for protection. Breeches, carriage tops and windows, shoes, bellows, boots, saddles, containers for liquids and dry goods, and harnesses are all examples of colonial leather products.

Settlers couldn't always wait for shipments of leather

"Unhairing" was one of the first steps an apprentice leatherworker learned. Low fires were kept burning night and day in the smokeroom until the hides began to rot and the hair became loose.

products to arrive from England. Many farmers began to operate tanneries. However, the leather they made was often of poor quality. It eventually became law that only professional tanners could make leather. This was done to protect the integrity of American leather and leather products. Even among the professionals, techniques and quality of leather varied.

The quality of leather could be affected by the species of the animal, its age, and its sex. Even the body part the pelt once covered was important. Tanners called the pelts of large animals like cattle and oxen hides. The pelts of smaller animals like sheep and deer were known as skins. Curing and tanning processes were used alone or in combination. Once pelts were tanned, they became known as leather.

The first step in leathermaking was to mark the pelt with the owner's initials. Heavy hides were cut into two pieces for easier handling. Any worthless ends were cut away. If the hide had been salted to preserve it, the tanner washed the salt and other dirt from it. He soaked the hide until it was soft and pliable. He also had to remove unwanted hair from it by using one of two methods: "liming" and "sweating."

In liming, powdered limestone and seashells are mixed in a tub of water. The hide is submerged. Bacteria builds up and causes the hair to loosen. After several days of soaking, the hide is removed from the water and allowed to drain.

Sweating could be done by simply stacking wet hides on top of each other. Or the process could be done in a smokehouse where apprentices kept low fires burning. In either case, after several days, the hides begin to rot and the hair becomes loose.

When the hairs could be removed easily, the tanner flung the hide over a "beam." A beam was a log split in half lengthwise. Its top surface was perfectly rounded and smoothed. The tanner used a two-handled unhairing knife to scrape the hair and the outer layer of skin (epidermis) from the grain side of the hide. The layer of skin that was left exposed was the corium. It was fibrous and full of gelatin. The gelatin would later combine chemically with the tanning agents to produce leather.

The craftsperson flipped the hide over. He used another two-handled fleshing knife to remove any fat or tissue that remained on the flesh side. He skived the hide to a uniform thickness for an even tanning. This technique resembled the shaving of wood with a plane. The skin was thoroughly washed in water or soaked in a solution of bate to remove all traces of lime. The hide was now ready for the tanning pits.

Tanning pits were huge tubs about six feet long, four feet deep, and four feet wide. They were sunk into the ground and separated by walkways. Each one was filled with "ooze," a mixture of water and a tanning bark. Tanning barks were any number of tree barks that contained tannin. This acid, also found in plants and leaves, prevented the cured and cleaned hides from further rotting. Black oak and hemlock were the most popular tanning barks.

After the hides were dumped into the tanning pits, the apprentices got to work. The boys would stir the hides many times. This prevented any ooze that was in contact with the hides from becoming weak and less effective. Occasionally, the hides were lifted from the pits and allowed to drain. The stirring, draining, and adding of tanning bark could go on for one to two years. It was difficult, strenuous labor.

A master tanner knew by the "feel" of his leather when it was ready to be removed from the tanning pit. Less experienced tanners would cut off a piece of hide. When it was brown all the way through, it was leather.

The leather was lifted from the pit and carted off to a stream for another washing. If all the ooze was not removed from the leather, it would continue acting, eventually weakening the fiber of the leather. A tanner's reputation depended on the quality of leather he produced. He would have to do some fast talking if a saddle made from his product fell apart, dumping the rider onto Main Street.

After the tanner skived the hide and cleaned
it of all bate, it was ready for the tanning pit.

Tanning processes varied for different leathers.
Calfskin or buckskin was prepared for tanning the same
way cowhide was. However, the skins were soaked in a
solution of hen or pigeon droppings, and only for seven
to ten days. This stinky procedure was followed by a six-
month soaking in increasingly stronger solutions of
ooze. The skins were frequently turned and handled.

Here a Native American leatherworker uses
traditional tanning methods and rubs a
deerskin with animal brains to soften it.

When they were leather, it was probably the poor apprentices who had to wash them.

Lighter skins like sheep, goat, and sometimes buckskin, were tawed. Tawing was a tanning process that
used a mixture of alum, salt, and water instead of ooze.

The leather produced by tawing was referred to as white leather. It was easily dyed and used for clothing or gloves.

Rawhide is not leather. It is a treated skin that can be much stronger than leather. Colonists used it for lacing, buckets, baskets, and similar items. The tanner cured the skins as he did hides. Then he punched holes along the outside of the skin. While it was wet, it was stretched and tied to a frame using rope or lacing. It was left to dry away from the sun and heat.

The finishing of leather was called currying. In the early colonies, the tanner was also the currier.

The currier's job was to make leather soft and pliable. Tired apprentices sighed with relief as they gave the leather its last soaking. Any rough or thick spots were trimmed from the flesh side. Yellow spots, called bloom, were removed from the grain side using a tool that resembled a grooved rolling pin. Both sides of the skin were scrubbed, then rubbed with a smooth stone set in a handle. The currier might have burnished the surface with a slicker. This was a dull piece of iron set in a thick oblong handle. He rubbed the leather with a blend of tanner's oil and tallow. He beat this in with a knobbed mallet called a mace. Sometimes the currier continued to oil the leather and buff it with pumice. Oiling and buffing brought out the leather's natural grain and color. It also added luster.

Very skillful tanners were responsible for making parchment and vellum. Parchment came from the untanned skins of sheep, lambs, and goats. Vellum was usually made from untanned calfskin. It had an excellent writing surface.

Turning hides and skins into leather was just as difficult as the building of a new nation. It is symbolic in many ways that vellum, not paper, was chosen when the American founders wrote the Declaration of Independence and the Constitution of the United States.

Source Notes

CHAPTER 1

1. Smith, Abbot Emerson. *Colonists in Bondage* (New York: W. W. Norton, 1947), p. 150. Original information from Winthrop's "Journal," published circa 1650.

CHAPTER 6

1. Cabell, Eleanor Kelly. *Women Milliners in 18th-Century Williamsburg* (Williamsburg, Virginia: Williamsburg Research Papers, 1988).

Glossary

adz an extremely sharp ax shaped like a hoe

alloy a substance composed of two or more metals or of a metal and a nonmetal united by being fused together and dissolved in each other when molten

anneal to heat, then slowly cool a metal to make it less brittle

anvil a heavy iron block on which metal is shaped

apprentice a person bound to serve another for a specified period with the intention of learning a trade; the first step in becoming a craftsperson

armorer in the colonies, the person responsible for repairing, assembling, or testing the local militia's guns

artificer a craftsperson

artisan (craftsperson) a person skilled in a manual craft

bar iron wrought iron formed into bars for storage

bate a solution used to remove lime from hides during the tanning process

battery in metalworking, the first hammering process

used to form sheet or plate metal; in hatmaking, the brick enclosed kettle where hats are boiled as they are planked

bellows an accordion-like instrument that draws air in through a valve and expels it through a tube

bloom spongy mass of molten iron

bloomery a simple ironworks for making wrought iron

borax a cleansing agent

braze to solder thin pieces of iron together

Britannia a female figure representing Great Britain

British lion passant a symbol of Great Britain; a crowned, walking lion with his forepaw raised

broadside a wooden frame wall for the side of a building

caliper an instrument with curved legs used for measuring thickness, diameter, or distance between surfaces

case shallow tray used to hold type

cast to give shape to molten metal by pouring it into a mold and allowing it to cool and harden

caul the net foundation for a wig

chaisemaker a craftsperson who makes any type of light two-wheeled or four-wheeled carriage that was usually open and seated one or two people

compositor the person in the printing shop who sets the type

cooper one who makes or repairs barrels, casks, buckets, and similar items

course a continuous line or row of bricks

crown molding a decorative wooden border that separates the wall from the ceiling

crucible a graphite bowl used for holding silver while it is being melted

date assayed the date a piece of English silver plate was appraised according to standards

devils apprentice printers

die a cast or hard metal pattern used for stamping or

cutting out some object; one of a pair of such patterns (one cameo and one intaglio) between which a piece of metal is embossed

drawing or **drawing out** lengthening or widening of metal

drawknife any number of two-handled, thin-bladed knives used by various craftspeople for different chores; a drawing knife could have a special name depending on its use; i.e. "fleshing knife" was a draw-knife used for fleshing skins and hides

dressing trimming rough projections from masonry material; in wigmaking, adjusting curls, combing, and adding ornaments and perfume to a wig

dry wall a stone wall requiring no cementing material

ductile able to be drawn out, bent, or hammered into thin sheets

farrier an ironworker who shoes horses and oxen

fillet a hand-held tool with a small wheel engraved with a repeating pattern, used for decorating leather in bookbinding

finial an ornamental knob usually placed on top of an item

flask a wooden frame used to hold sand molds

fleshing to remove fat, flesh, and gristle from a hide or skin

fleshing beam a smooth, rounded beam used when scraping a hide

fleshing knife a drawknife with a slightly curved blade used for fleshing

flux to cleanse by removing oxides from metal; to promote melting and fusing of metals

forge to heat and shape hot metals; a furnace for heating metals

freedom dues gifts an apprentice received from the master at the end of his or her servitude

fuse to melt and blend, creating a bond

girts end beams used in construction

glazier a craftsperson who made glass

graphite black lead

hackle a fine-tooth comb

hallmark the symbol of the guild hall where pieces of English silver were appraised

housewright one who builds houses

indenture a contract binding one person to work for another for a set length of time

ingot a bar of silver or gold

intaglio engraved printing

joinery the craft of joining pieces of wood together to form paneled doors, wainscoting, floors, window and door frames, and furniture

jointer a large floor plane with a sharp exposed edge

journeyman/journeywoman a paid worker who has completed the apprenticeship requirements

lathe a machine used by a craftsperson to hold and rotate his work while he guides it along a cutting tool to shape it

limestone rock formed mainly of organic remains; yields lime when burned

maker's mark the trade symbol of a smith

malleable able to be rolled or hammered without breaking

mantua-maker a dressmaker

masonry work performed using stone, rock, marble, brick, and cementing materials

milliner a dressmaker who sold ready-made and custom-made garments, along with a "thousand other things"

millwork carpentry work made off-site that is ready for installation when it is delivered

mortar a mixture of sand and lime

nonporous something that does not have pores and will not absorb liquid

pelt an animal skin or hide with hair still on it

planish to polish

pot hook an iron collar sometimes worn by runaway indentured servants who were captured

pumice volcanic rock or ash used for polishing

rawhide treated, but untanned, animal skin prepared by stretching and dry curing

refine to remove impurities

rottenstone soft rock used to burnish metal

sawyer one who saws logs

shipsmith a blacksmith who specializes in nautical items

silver plate term used for silver products because they were fashioned from a flat plate of silver

skiving shaving leather to a uniform thickness

slag impurities removed from iron during smelting

swage a form used for shaping metal by hammering or applying pressure

symmetrical having parts on one side that correspond or match identically those on the other side

tawing treating skins with alum and water

turning a wooden or metal item shaped on a lathe

wrought iron refined iron containing very little carbon

Bibliography

Aitchison, Leslie. *A History of Metals*, 2nd Volume. New York: 1960.

Alderman, Clifford Lindsey. *Colonists for Sale.* New York: Macmillan, 1975.

Anderson, Bonnie and Judith P. Zinssler. *A History of Their Own*, Vols. I & II. New York: Harper and Row, 1988, 1989.

Aptheker, Herbert. *The Colonial Era.* New York: International Publishers, 1966.

Ballagh, James Curtis. *White Servitude in the Colony of Virginia.* New York: Burt Franklin, 1895, reprinted 1969.

Churchill, James. *The Complete Book of Tanning Skins and Furs.* Harrisburg, Pennsylvania: Stackpole Books, 1983.

Coffin, Margaret. *The History and Folklore of American Country Tinware.* Camden, New Jersey: Thomas Nelson & Sons, 1988.

Earle, Alice Morse. *Home Life In Colonial Days.* Stock-

bridge, Massachusetts: Macmillan, 1898; reprinted
by Grosset & Dunlap, New York, 1974.

Farnham, Albert B. *Home Tanning and Leather Making Guide*. Columbus, Ohio: A. R. Harding, 1950.

Fisher, Leonard Everett. *The Architects*. New York: Franklin Watts, 1970.

_____. *The Blacksmiths*. New York: Franklin Watts, 1976.

_____. *The Cabinetmakers*. New York: Franklin Watts, 1966.

_____. *The Hatters*. New York: Franklin Watts, 1965.

_____. *The Papermakers*. New York: Franklin Watts, 1965.

_____. *The Printers*. New York: Franklin Watts, 1965.

_____. *The Silversmiths*. New York: Franklin Watts, 1964.

_____. *The Tanners*. New York: Franklin Watts, 1966.

_____. *The Wigmakers*. New York: Franklin Watts, 1965.

Fletcher, Sir Banister. *A History of Architecture*, 15th Edition. London, England: B. T. Batsford, Ltd., 1950.

Fradin, Dennis B. *The Pennsylvania Colony*. Chicago, Illinois: Childrens Press, 1988.

Gromley, Myrna Vanderpool. "Colonial Love and Marriage," *Colonial Homes Magazine*. October, 1990.

Heirloom Bible. *Labor and the Bible*. Wichita, Kansas: Heirloom Bible Publishers, 1987.

Hogg, Garry. *Hammer and Tongs: Blacksmithing Down the Ages*, London, England: Hutchinson Co., 1964.

Honeychurch, Douglas. "Molding Character: Using a Molder/Planer on Site to Create 18th Century Interior." *Fine Homebuilding Magazine*, June/July, 1987, No. 40.

Kauffman, Henry J. *The American Pewterer, His Techniques and His Products*. Camden, New Jersey: Thomas Nelson, Inc., 1970.

_____. *The Colonial Silversmith, His Techniques and His Products.* Camden, New Jersey: Thomas Nelson, Inc., 1969.

Kellogg, Kathy. *Home Tanning and Leathercraft Simplified.* Charlotte, Vermont: Williamson Publishing Co., 1984.

Knauth, Percy. *The Metalsmiths.* New York: Time-Life Books, 1974.

Lister, Raymond. *The Craftsmen in Metal.* Cranbury, New Jersey: A.S. Barnes & Co., 1968.

Montgomery, Charles. *A History of American Pewter.* New York: E. P. Dutton, 1973, 1978.

The New Book of Knowledge. Danbury, Connecticut: Grolier, Inc.

"Guns and Ammunition," Eldon G. Wolff, Curator, History Department, Milwaukee Public Museum, 1989, Vol 7, pp. 414–426.

"Bookbinding," Margaret Saul, R. R. Bowker Co., Vol 2B, pp. 327–329.

"Books," Richard W. Ireland, Vol 2B, pp. 318–322.

"Brick and Masonry," Carl W. Conduit, Vol 2B, pp. 390–394.

North, Anthony and Ian V. Hogg. *The Book of Guns and Gunsmiths.* London, England: Quartro Ltd., New Burlington Books, 1977.

Pope, Dudley. *Guns From the Invention of Gun Powder to the Twentieth Century.* London, England: George Weidenfeld & Nicholson, Ltd., New York: Delacorte Press, 1965.

Reich, Jerome R. *Colonial America.* Englewood Cliffs, New Jersey: Prentice-Hall, 1984.

Sichel, Marion. *Costume Reference, Volume 4: Eighteenth Century.* Boston, Massachusetts: Plays, Inc., 1977.

Simpson, Bruce J. *History of the Metalcasting Industry.* Des Plaines, Illinois: American Foundrymen's Society, Inc., 1969.

Smith, Abbot Emerson. *Colonists in Bondage: White Servitude and Convict Labor in America, 1607–1776.* Glouster, Massachusetts: Peter Smith, 1965.

Tunis, Edwin. *Colonial Craftsmen and the Beginning of American Industry.* Cleveland, Ohio: The World Publishing Co., 1965.

————. *Colonial Living.* Cleveland, Ohio: The World Publishing Co., 1957.

Wamsley, James. *The Crafts of Williamsburg.* Williamsburg, Virginia: The Colonial Williamsburg Foundation, 1982.

Welsh, Kenneth E. *The History of Clocks and Watches.* New York: Drake Publishers, Inc., 1972.

Williamsburg Craft Series:

DeMatteo, William. *The Silversmith in Eighteenth-Century Williamsburg.* Williamsburg, Virginia: Colonial Williamsburg Foundation, 1956.

Ford, Thomas K., based on unpublished studies by Harold B. Gill, Jr. and Raymond Townsend. *The Leatherworker in Eighteenth-Century Williamsburg.* Williamsburg, Virginia: Colonial Williamsburg Foundation, 1967.

Ford, Thomas K., based on an unpublished monograph by Mills Brown. *The Cabinetmaker in Eighteenth-Century Williamsburg.* Williamsburg, Virginia: Colonial Williamsburg Foundation, 1970.

Williamsburg Research Papers:

Cabell, Eleanor Kelly. "Women Milliners in 18th Century Williamsburg." Williamsburg, Virginia: Opus Publications, Inc., 1988.

Gill, Harold B. "Blacksmiths in Colonial Williamsburg." Williamsburg, Virginia: Opus Publications, 1965.

Townsend, Raymond R. "Apprenticeship in Colonial Williamsburg." (From Study Manual #2) Williamsburg, Virginia: Opus Publications, 1960.

Wright, Esmond. *Franklin of Philadelphia.* Cambridge, Massachusetts: Belknap Press of Harvard University, 1986.

Wright, Louis B. *Everyday Life in Colonial America.* New York: G. P. Putnam's Sons, 1965.

Wroth, Lawrence C. *The Colonial Printer.* Charlottesville, Virginia: Dominion Books, 1964.

INTERVIEWS

Agne, Jim: expert woodworker and reenactor who specializes in the colonial period using antique tools and reproductions of antique tools of colonial woodworkers

Alonzo, Joe: master stonemason on site, National Cathedral, Washington, D.C.

Brown, Richard: architect, Fairfax, Virginia

Ennis, William Richard: master marblemason, Raleigh, North Carolina

Fleister, Andy: farrier, Laurel, Maryland

Gardner, Dan: farrier, Prince Georges County, Maryland

Gussler, Wallace: master gunsmith, Williamsburg, Virginia

Kindig, Earl M.: grandson of Daniel W. Kindig, cabinetmaker, Bethlehem, Pennsylvania

McNey, Bob: journeyman carpenter, Galbreath Company, Fairfax, Virginia

Scokul, Edward: master gunsmith, Long Island, New York

Smith, Danny: journeyman carpenter, Galbreath Company, Fairfax, Virginia

For Further Reading

Fisher, Leonard Everett. *The Architects.* New York: Franklin Watts, 1970.
———. *The Blacksmiths.* New York: Franklin Watts, 1976.
———. *The Glassmakers.* New York: Franklin Watts, 1966.
———. *The Potters.* New York: Franklin Watts, 1969.
———. *The Shipbuilders.* New York: Franklin Watts, 1971.
———. *The Shoemakers.* New York: Franklin Watts, 1967.
———. *The Weavers.* New York: Franklin Watts, 1966.
———. *The Wigmakers.* New York: Franklin Watts, 1965.
Kauffman, Henry J. *The Colonial Silversmith, His Techniques and His Products.* Camden, New Jersey: Thomas Nelson, Inc., 1969.
Tunis, Edwin. *Colonial Craftsmen and the Beginning of*

American Industry. Cleveland, Ohio: The World Publishing Co., 1965, 1972.

_____. *Colonial Living*. Cleveland, Ohio: The World Publishing Co., 1957.

Wamsley, James. *The Crafts of Williamsburg*. Williamsburg, Virginia: The Colonial Williamsburg Foundation, 1982.

Index

Page numbers in *italics* indicate illustrations.

Adz, 40
Alloy, 58, 63, 66, 69
America, 21, 23, 50, 74, 89, 99
American Revolution, 12
"Antenuptial contract," 90
Anvil, 60, 61, 62, *65*, 67, 69, 77, 79
Apprentices, 11–19, *16*, 74, *86*, 99
   abuse of, 19
   education of, 12, 13, 16, 17, 92
   female, 13, 17, 92

   freedom dues, 12, 15, 17, 19
   runaway, 17, 19
   trepanning of, 13, 15
   vows, 12
Aquafortis, 72
Architects, 31, 32–35
"Ardent Desire of the Deceased," 56

Bar iron, 74, 77, 78
Barrels, 21
Bellows, 57, 58, 67, 74, 77, 103
Bible, the, 17, 54
Blacksmiths, 23, *59*, 62, 64, 73–79
   apprentices, 78

Bloomery, 74
Bookbinders, 52–56,
  55
Bookbinding, 50, 52, 54
Brass, 70, 78, 81
Brick houses, 32
Bricklayers, 31, 35, 37–
  40, *86*
    apprentices, *38*, 40
Bronze, 72, 84
Builders, 31–44, *41*
    apprentices, 31, 33

Cabinetmakers, 23–30,
  28, 44, 70
    apprentices, 24, 25,
    26, 27
Candle making, *18*
Carlyle, Thomas, 45, 56
Carpenters, 20, 27, 29,
  30, *30*, 40–44, *41*, *43*,
  75, 82
Carvers, 30
Caulkers, *30*
Chairbacks, *28*
Chaisemakers, 30
Charleston, S.C., 24
Chasing, 63
Child labor laws, 15
Chippendale, Thomas,
  24, 25
Clocks, 64, 70
Clock making, 70
Coachmakers, 29
Coins, 65, 66, 83, 84
Composing stick, 51
Compositors, 50, 51, *51*

Coopers, 20, 21–23, 22,
  29, *30*
    apprentices, 22
Constitution of the
  United States, 109
Coping tool, 36
Copper, 66, 70, 84,
  85
Couchers, 46, *49*
Crucible, 67
Currier, 109
    apprentices, 109
Currying, 109
Cutlers, 73, 81–82
Cutters of punches and
  dies, 83

Damascening, 70
Declaration of
  Independence, 109
Dentists, 64
Dies, 83
Drawing, 77, 78, 79
Drawing out, 62, 63
Dressmakers, 89, 90, 92,
  93, 94

Embossed stamps, 83,
  84
England, 19, 20, 32, 33,
  45, 50, 94, 98, 104
English Law, 12
English Parliament, 77,
  97
Engraved printing, 83–
  84
Engraving, 61, 63, 70

Family Well-Ordered, A (Mather), 54, 55
Farriers, 73, 79–80, *80*
Felt, 94
Felting process, 97
Filigree, 69
Fillet, 54
Finish, 29
Finishers, 97
First Amendment, 56
Fleshing knife, 106
Forge, 57, 58, 66
Founders, 82, 84
Franklin, Benjamin, *14*
French Revolution, 102
Fulling process, 95
Fur, 95, 97
Furniture, 20, 23, 24, 25, *25*, 27, 29

Galley, 52
Galley proof, 50, 52
Gentleman and Cabinetmaker's Director, The (Chippendale), 24
Geometry, 24, 72
Gilding, 82
Glassmakers, *86*
Glaziers, 44, 70
Glue, 27
Gold, 54, 64, 69, 70, 72, 82
Gold beating, 70
Gold leafing, 70
Goldsmiths, 61, 64, 66, 69–71, *71*, 72
Guilds, 12, 13

Gunsmiths, *76*

Hat Act of 1731, 97
Hatmakers, 94–98, *96*
  apprentices, 97
Henry Francis Dupont Winterthur Museum, 25
Hewers, *30*, 40, *41*
Hollowware, 68
Home building, *33*
Hurl, 95, *96*

Indentured servants, 11, 17, 19, 89
Indentures, 11, 12, 15, 19
Industrial Revolution, 87
Inlaying, 69
Iron, 73, 74, 75, *75*, 77, 81, 82
Iron Act of 1750, 77
Iron foundries, 82
Iron industry, 74, 77
Ironworkers, 60, 73, 74, 77, 82

Jamestown, Virginia, 74, 89
Japanning, 72
Jewelry, 64, 69, 71
Joiners, 20, 23–30, *30*, 44, 82
Jointer, 22, 23
Joints, 27, 28
Joist, 25, 42

Journeymen, 15, 50
Journeywomen, 92

Lacemaking, bobbin, *91*
Lacquering, 72
Lathes, 26, 61
    treadle, 26, 85
    great wheel, 26, 85
Leather products, 23, 54,
    85, 97, 103, 104, 105
Leatherworkers, 103–9,
    104, 108
"Legacy for
    Children . . . , A," 56
Letterpress, *51*, 52
"Liming," 105
Log cabins, 32
London, England, 13,
    50, 66
Long pit saw, 40

Mantua-makers, 92. *See
    also* Dressmakers
Marble masons, 35
Mashing hammer, 36
Masonry, 35
Masons, 35–37
    apprentices, 35
Master craftspeople, 12,
    15, 16, *16*, 17, 19, 33,
    38
Mather, Cotton, 54, 55
Mayflower, 89
Metal casting, 63, 67, 69,
    82, 83
Metal casts, 84
Metalworkers, 57–87

apprentices, 57
Milliners, 89–94, *93*, 97
Milliner's agent, 94
Molder, 82
Molds, 63, 84
    sand, 61, 63, 82
    skillet, 67
    slush, 84
    two-piece cast-iron
        ingot, 67
Mortar, 37, *38*, 39
Mourning rings, 69

Native Americans, 31,
    62, 68, 74, 108
Needlework, 89, 92
New England, 19, 54
Newport, R.I., 24
Notary stamp, 84

Papermakers, 46–48, *49*
    apprentices, 46
Papermills, 46, *47, 49*
Parchment, 109
Patternmakers, 82
Pewter, 84, 85
Pewterers, 84–85
Pewterware, 84
Philadelphia, Penn., 24,
    56, 102
Pirates, 65
Pitching tool, 36
Pitmen, 40, 44
Planishing hammer, *49*,
    69
Plating hammer, 48
Poor Law of 1601, 13

Poor Law of 1672, 13
"Pot hook," 17
Printers, 48–52, 53, 83
  apprentices, 50
Punches, 61, 77, 81,
  83

Ragpickers, 46. *See also*
  Papermakers'
  apprentices
Raising hammer, 69
Ramillies wig, 99
Rawhide, 109
Repoussé, 61, 63
Revere, Paul, 72
Rottenstone, 69, 85

Sash saw, 40
Sawyers, 29, *30*, 40, 44
Sewing, 17, 89, 90, 92
Shingle-makers, 44
Shipbuilding, *30*
Shipsmiths, 73
  apprentices, 73
Silver, 54, 64, 65, 66, 67,
  68, 69, 70, 72, 78
Silverplate, 64, 66
Silversmiths, 64–72, *65*,
  68, 77
  apprentices, 66, 67 /
Slaves, 98
Smelting, 58, 81
Smiths, 44, 57, 84
Snarling tools, 77
Solder, 63, 69, 78
Spirit level, 39
Stamping mills, 46

Statute of Artificers of
  1563, 13
Steel-die printing, 83–
  84. *See also* Engraved
  printing
Steeling, 81
Sterling silver, 66
Stone carving, 35
Stonemasons, 35, 36
Summer beams, 25
Surveyors, *34*
Swages, 61, 77
"Sweating," 105

Tanneries, 104
Tanners, 75, 103–9,
  107
  apprentices, 105,
    106, 108
Tanning, 103, 106, 107,
  107
Tanning bark, 106
Tanning pits, 106,
  107
Tanning processes,
  105, 107, *107*,
  108
Tawing, 108, 109
Tin, 72, 73, 84, 85
"Tin cry," 73
Tinkers, 85–87
Tin plague, 73
Tricornered hats, 94
Two-handled float, 85
Type, 48, 50, 51, 52, 83,
  84
Type foundries, 50

Undertakers, 30
Unhairing knife, *104*, 105
Upholstery work, 30
Upsetting, 77, 79

Vatmen, 46, 49
Vellum, 52, 109
Virginia Company, 13,
19, 74

Wafer irons, 83
Washington, George, *34*, 102
Welding, 60, 77, 78, 79,
81

White leather, 109
Whitesmiths, 23, 72–73
Wigmakers, 98–102,
100
Wigs, 94, 98, 99, 101,
102
Woodworkers, 20–30, 25,
82
Worshipful Company of
Goldsmiths of the City
of London, 66

Yarn spinning, *18*
Yorktown, Virginia, 15